PRAISES FOR
THE PAIN BEHIND MY SMILE

There are not enough words to describe how proud I am of you for finally choosing YOU. Throughout my whole life, I have watched you put others first by making sure everyone is fine. You have chosen yourself and your happiness for the first time. I am sure it wasn't an easy decision, but it was definitely worth it. You are an amazing woman, daughter and mother, and I am so thankful to have you in my life at all times.
        -Catina Hernandez, Cousin

The strength you show everyday inspires me to fight through any situation that comes my way. When I doubt myself and think I can't handle some challenges, your inspiration gives me hope. The compassion you have for people really shows what a wonderful heart you have. You are never afraid to stand your ground, and I admire you for that. I have always needed a friend who's not afraid to tell me how it is, and GOD brought me you.

-Sarah Gordon, Best Friend

I love you and admire your courage to share your story. The Pain Behind My Smile is a story of love, sacrifice, growth and freedom. It will give you the strength to find your voice and know your worth. A strong woman's tale.

-Janine Smith, Best Friend

And eventually, every woman discovers
the power to heal herself.

the pain behind my smile

A story of discovering triumph amidst truth.

MELISSA TRINCHET

The Pain Behind My Smile. Melissa Trinchet. All rights reserved. No part of this publication may be reproduced, distributed, or transmitted in any form or by any means, including photocopying, recording, or other electronic or mechanical methods, without the prior written permission of the publisher, except in the case of brief quotations embodied in critical reviews and certain other noncommercial uses permitted by copyright law. For permission requests, write to the publisher, addressed:

> "Attention: Permissions Coordinator,"
> 500 N. Michigan Avenue, Suite
> 600, Chicago, IL 60611.

13th & Joan books may be purchased for educational, business or sales promotional use. For information, please email the Sales Department at sales@13thandjoan.com.

Printed in the U.S. A.

First Printing, June 2018
Library of Congress Cataloging-in-Publication Data has been applied for.

ISBN: 978-1-7324712-3-8

Dedication

This book is gratefully dedicated to my loving Mother, the late Linda D. Trinchet, who inspired me to write my first book. I appreciate how you raised me and all the love that you gave me. You are the wind beneath my wings. I love and miss you dearly.

Acknowledgements

First and foremost, I want to thank God for saving me during my darkest moments and for never giving up on me. You are truly awesome! I would like to thank my amazing publishing company, 13th & Joan, who pushed me, from the beginning to the end, to write this book. A special thank you to Ardre Orie for her guidance and patience through my writing process. Most importantly, I thank you for giving me the opportunity to share my story.

I would like to thank my family and my friends who have supported me through the old and new journey of my life. A heartfelt thank you is sent to four special people in my life, Joyce, Chad, Shelby & Jon. Each of you played a huge part in my book by guiding me with ideas; you felt my pain during my writing, and gave generous donations to make sure I reached my fundraising goal to publish my book. You have no idea how much I appreciate each of you, and I can't thank you enough for your love and support! I would like to thank my friends who also donated to help me reach my fundraising goal.

Thank you to my amazing support system, you know who you are. The past year was very difficult for me, but I made up my mind that I would get through it. I did it with great pride! Thank you to my first born nephew and niece who were there for me every step of the way by reading my draft and giving me advice and suggestions. I love you both dearly. Last, but not least, I want to thank my children. My handsome sons, the protection and love that both of you have for me is the greatest gift a mother could imagine. I love you both with all of my heart. To my beautiful daughter, I thank you for being my rock, and for giving me advice when I read a chapter to you and for hugging me every time you saw me crying. Your warm hugs assured me that everything would be okay. Your unconditional love and support during my healing process and your patience through my writing have been truly amazing. I can't thank you enough for being my number #1 fan. I love you with everything, Sunflower!

The strong ones always survive. Where there is darkness, there is light.

    -Melissa Trinchet

Introduction

Thank you for purchasing my book and for supporting my new journey! As you begin to read my book, I would like to share with you what motivated me to write, "*The Pain Behind My Smile*". When I was in my early twenties, my Mother, who was my everything and with whom I shared everything, told me if I were to ever write a book, others would be inspired through my experiences. She inspired me because she believed that my story would help others along their journey. When my Mother first told me this, I didn't think anything of it. One day, I was sitting on my front porch, and I started to think of all of the abuse and the affairs that I allowed myself to tolerate, while staying in an unhealthy, toxic marriage.

The title idea for my book came from the realization of the fake "happy" life that I was living while wearing a smile on my face. I was hiding the pain behind my smile. I struggled while making the final decision to tell my personal story, but I recognized that there are others like me who are living many of the same experiences that I went through and that my story could possibly heal or inspire in some way.

This is my story, and I own it! In my sharing, I received negative feedback from a small group of people who thought that I shouldn't share my story, and it created doubt within me. One person asked me, "Why are you sharing something so personal"? It's not ideal for everyone to know your business. My response was respectful because I'm not ashamed to tell my story when I know that my experiences will help others. We go through things in life, good and bad, to learn from them. Therefore, if you have the opportunity to share, then go for it! Don't let anyone judge you on your experiences; it's not for them to judge - always remember that! If you're afraid to tell your story, that's a good enough reason to share it. You do not deserve to live in shame or in fear of the consequences of sharing your truth. After you read my book, it is my hope that you take away positive messages to guide you towards the right direction along the journey to the happiness that you deserve.

Table of Contents

Prologue: Freedom Over the Illusion of Loyalty 1
1. Getting to Know Me 3
2. How We Met 9
3. Hurtful First Year 15
4. Depressed While Expecting 25
5. What was I Thinking? 31
6. The Affairs 37
7. Not Feeling Loved or Wanted 49
8. The Physical and Mental Abuse 53
9. The Cycles of Life 61
10. Facing the Lady in the Mirror 65
11. Praying by Kesha 67
12. Courage To Finally Leave 73
13. Reality 79
14. Letting Go 83

Daily Motivational Reads 87
Dear Self 88

Epilogue: A Penny for Your Thoughts	91
Dark Moment	93
My Favorite Cousin	96
Letters of Love	99
Dear Curtis	103
About the Author	107
Connect with Melissa Trinchet on Social Media	109

PROLOGUE
Freedom Over the Illusion of Loyalty

"Never wish them pain, wish them healing."
-Melissa Trinchet

As you read my book, you will experience mixed emotions because what I went through won't seem acceptable to you. It will make you wonder why I tolerated it for so long. I ask that you hear my heart and my story of a strong woman, who was finally brave enough to leave and who recognized her worth. I stayed with a man for twenty-three years whom I loved with all of my heart. I loved him more than I loved myself. However, during that twenty-three years, I was too blind to see that he didn't love me the way that I deserved to be loved. Sometimes, the one you're with for the longest time turns out to be the wrong one for you. I kept accepting less when I knew I deserved more. I stayed as long as I did, not because I was weak, but because I was hoping that he was going to change after each promise.

the pain behind my smile

I finally left because I realized that I no longer loved while loving him. Letting go means choosing freedom over the illusion of loyalty. I'm not ashamed for speaking my truth, it made me the strong woman I am today. I overcame the storm with the sun shining on me. My heart has been wounded, bruised, scarred, torn, broken, and even ripped apart. I've been battered, manipulated, and used, but my soul still loves and forgives. My heart remains authentic and true.

ONE
Getting to Know Me

"Don't be a prisoner of your past."
-Melissa Trinchet

Growing up as a child was bittersweet. I was born on May 23, 1975, in Alexandria, VA. At the time of my birth, there were complications that required immediate attention from the doctors and nurses. As of today, according to my Father and aunt, it's still not clear what happened to me. However, I do remember what my Mother told me which was-- I had to get blood transfusions. Due to my veins not being visible, both of my ankles were cut to get an IV in to get fluid going through my body. I was dehydrated, and I lost a lot of blood.

After that, my mother always kept me under her wing and always called me her miracle child. Growing up, there were happy moments at home, but most were sad. I can recall our small, three bedroom apartment with my Mother, Father, two brothers and sister. There were constant arguments between my Mother and Father over the rent and bills not being paid. My

Mother was always sad, with a red face that confirmed she had been crying. I eventually learned that my Father had a gambling problem. There were times when my Mother had to ask her parents to pay the rent, or ask them for Christmas money to get us a few things to put a smile on our faces. There were times when my Mother had to work double shifts at work to fill in the financial gaps when my Father failed to pull his weight. My Mother was exhausted from working so many hours, and I felt badly for her.

In elementary school, my good days consisted of going to school and playing with my friends. When I came home from school, I most often stayed at home. I wanted to stay near my Mother. As I moved on to middle school, I started to hang out with my friends after school. I started to get into cheerleading, and I really enjoyed it. After moving on to high school, I played basketball my freshman year, and then I tried out for the cheerleading team and made the varsity team. This was an exciting time for me, as I really enjoyed being a teenager. When my siblings and I were younger, we were all very close. My brothers were very protective of me, and my sister was extremely protective of me.

My Mother always dressed my sister and I alike in dresses, and she also dressed my brothers alike. We captured a lot of those special moments, as my Mother enjoyed taking pictures of us. Her children were her pride and joy! I currently have a close relationship with my two brothers, but I am not as close with my sister. I hear from her once, or twice a week, with short conversations. I miss the close relationship I once had with my sister. I watched the fast lifestyle she lived, along with doing drugs and being an alcoholic. These things took a toll on her life.

I then stepped in to help my mother raise my sister's two children, while everyone kept making excuses as to why my sister didn't come home, or why she worked so much. I was the little sister that always looked up to her, and I wanted to be like her when we were growing up. Regardless of how that experience impacted me, I will always love my sister the same. I also have two older siblings that were from my Father's previous marriage. I met them once or twice when I was younger. None of us have a close relationship with them; we only communicate through Facebook here and there.

The relationship between my Mother and Father wasn't good at all. My Mother always told me that she was only staying with my father for us. When I got older and felt that I could ask, I inquired about her leaving my Father. She said she couldn't afford it because he made more money that was used to support us. Sadly, I barely ever saw my Mother happy. I was present for most of the arguments between my Mother and my Father. I can remember when he would come home drunk and start arguments by pushing her when she would walk away from him. As this continued, my parents ended up sleeping in separate rooms, and the arguments continued. There were times when my parents didn't speak to each other while being under the same roof. My Mother continued to cook dinner every day, clean, and wash clothes, while trying to keep the peace. We knew she was doing it for us.

Eventually, my Mother felt that she could not stay in the marriage, and she ended up moving out of the home and moved in with my sister. I can remember that day like it was yesterday. I was twenty-three years old, and I had just had my second son. I cried like a baby when she moved out. This was the hardest adjustment for me, but in the back of my mind I knew that I had to stop being selfish, and understand why my Mother made the decision to leave. She didn't leave because of us. She left because she was mentally drained from what she was going through with my Father, and she was tired of not being happy.

My Mother divorced my Father, and five months later, my Father married a young, Brazilian woman. This was very hard for us to accept, because the divorce of my parents was still fresh in our minds. For my Father to move on as quickly as he did was a huge shock. He had no remorse for how much their divorce impacted us with so much hurt. The relationship between my Mother and Father went downhill, as my Mother felt that my Father's new wife was already in the picture while they were still together. It took a year or so before my parents were cordial with each other. My Mother never got an apology from my Father for what she went through.

I have always had a close-knit family. There were family gatherings, such as cookouts, birthday parties, and weddings that kept us all connected. The unexpected passing of my Mother is what disconnected our family. My Mother suffered her third heart attack at the young age of fifty-one. This was by far the hardest thing I had to experience; I was in total shock! My Mother meant everything to me. She was there for me up until the day she passed away. She wasn't just my mother; she was my best friend. I am truly blessed to have shared an amazing relationship with her. We were inseparable, and our bond was unbreakable.

I was there with my Mother from the day she called me for help, because she was having symptoms of a heart attack. I stayed with her until the day she passed. On January 1, 2003 at 12:01a.m., my Mother took her last breath. Her passing took a huge toll on our family as everyone was in disbelief and started to distance themselves. My Mother was the glue that kept the family together. She always planned the family gatherings to make sure we all remained close. The distance in our family came about because no one wanted to step in and take my Mother's place. We found ourselves arguing back and forth about where to spend Christmas and Thanksgiving and where to have dinner on those special holidays. A few months after the passing of my Mother, my brother, his wife and kids moved away. A year later, I moved away with Curtis and the kids. And, a year later after that, my Father moved to the same county as my brother and I.

After the passing of my Mother, my Father and I became close. Today, my Father lives with a lot of guilt for how badly he treated my Mother. Even though my Father didn't treat my Mother like he should have, he's still my Father, and I knew that I had to forgive him, and move on. We now have the best relationship, and he's an amazing grandfather to my three children. I wouldn't trade him for the world!

The other relevant character who played a huge part in my teenage life was my high school boyfriend. He was my first love, but we had a crazy relationship that consisted of him cheating and physically abusing me. I was in that relationship for three years; the relationship ended due to his infidelity. Shortly after that, I rebounded into another relationship that only lasted a few months. This guy ended up being abusive, and he cheated on me numerous times. I had to leave that relationship when he punched me in the jaw, and I moved away. Being in these two abusive and cheating relationships, as well as seeing my

Father put my Mother through the same thing, I was impacted in my marriage.

I continued to accept Curtis' behavior for many reasons. I had grown up witnessing the same kind of behavior in my Mother's marriage, and I had experienced it in two of my previous relationships. Desperately, I wanted to believe that Curtis was different and that he loved me enough to change. Having watched my Mother stay in an abusive marriage, resulted in my feeling that perhaps there was something normal about it, and I felt like this was one of the main reasons I stayed as long as I did. Deep down inside, I felt that I deserved to be treated differently, better, and this marriage wasn't normal or healthy. I had to admit that I was in denial.

As for my friends, I can count on one hand how many of them have had a positive impact in my life and those who have helped me get through the tough times. No matter what time of the day or night, or whatever they were doing, they were always there for me. Without the love and support of my family and friends, I really don't know how I would have made it through the tough times.

My outlook on life is about learning how to be humble and happy and to recognize my worth as a woman. My goal is to live the life I love, and to love the life I live. My life experiences have made me wiser, stronger and a better person. No matter what tough situation I face, I smile through it and thank God for my wonderful life. I will no longer tolerate disrespect, mental and physical abuse or cheating from a man. I have found my outlook on life. I shall live my life the best way that I can knowing that I am responsible for protecting my heart.

TWO

How We Met

"Always go with your gut feeling."
-Melissa Trinchet

In November 1993, I met Curtis through a close friend I went to high school with. Her name was Faith, and she said I needed to meet her cousin because we would be a perfect match for each other. Faith insisted on saying this because she knew how headstrong I was, and apparently, Curtis was the same way and needed to meet "his match". I was eighteen and Curtis was nineteen. Faith planned a date for us to meet, and when I met Curtis, he wasn't what I expected. We ended up going to a restaurant, and all I could remember is how immature Curtis and his friend were acting in the restaurant. As the night came to an end, Curtis offered to take me home instead of his cousin Faith. I hesitated a bit since I had just met him, but knowing he was my good friend's cousin, I trusted him to take me home. When we arrived at my house, we talked in the car for a while. As I was leaving out the car to go in the house,

Curtis asked for my phone number. From that day forward against my better judgement, we spent everyday together. I met his family, and we all connected right away. There was one family gathering that sparked a red flag, which was when I went with Curtis to his Grandmother's house for Thanksgiving. I remember sitting in the basement with Curtis watching his family play cards, and I felt the tension between Curtis and his Father. His Father would ask him questions and Curtis would short answer him with a rude attitude. As we were getting ready to leave for Curtis to take me home, his Father asked him what time he would be home, and his response to his Father was "I don't know, when I get there"! It's often said that you can tell how a person is by the way they treat their parents. Therefore, at this point, I wasn't liking what I was seeing with Curtis' behavior, along with how arrogant and rude he was. When we got in the car, I asked Curtis why he treated his father the way he does, and he said they don't have a good relationship because he didn't like who his father married, which was Curtis' high school counselor. However, throughout our time being together and I was around the family more, I noticed a positive difference between Curtis and his Father's interactions. I felt the difference in their relationship had a lot to do with my talks with Curtis about treating his Father better and because Curtis saw the close relationship I had with my Father. After two months of being together, I got a call from Faith asking how things were going between Curtis and I, and I told her things were going great and how happy I was. She told me Curtis called her earlier that day thanking her for introducing us and how much he likes me. He then told her that I was going to be his wife and the Mother of his children. Four months later, Curtis asked me to marry him because he was going into the military and didn't want to lose me. I happily accepted, and we got married in March, 1994. While this marriage took place, Curtis and I chose not to tell our parents and only told two of our close friends, including Faith. However, Curtis' Mother ended up finding out because Curtis' Father found a card in his bedroom that I had given Curtis, and I signed it-- "your wife". Curtis' Mother called me very upset and wanted us to get the marriage annulled, but we both told her "no." Eventually, they all accepted it since they couldn't tell us what to do because I was eighteen and Curtis was nineteen. After Curtis and I got married, I introduced him to the rest of my family and friends. I remember him commenting on how close my family was and how nice it was to have that type of relationship with my family. Months and years went by, and I start to notice Curtis' jealousy with my family and friends. My family had their own reservations about Curtis but never said much to me about it. Curtis didn't like me going anywhere with my friends, he said married women shouldn't go out with their friends. Therefore, to keep the peace, I barely went out and was home most of the time with Curtis and the kids. The only time I would go out was with someone in my family, his family or to one of our family functions. When I went to the store, I always had to take one of the kids with me because Curtis didn't want me to go anywhere by myself. Curtis' jealousy continued to times when he started complaining about my family coming over to our house; he said he wanted to move away.

 A mutual friend, who had just purchased a home, told us about a good realtor. As we started to look around for houses, Curtis mentioned moving away from my family because he was tired of them coming over all the time. Our realtor mentioned a county that was an hour away from where we were living, and Curtis immediately said, "yes, that's perfect"! I agreed as well, as I wanted to keep him happy and have no issues. Once we moved, I had grown to like the county and most importantly, my kids loved the area. We met some great friends, and the schools were great. Two years later, my brother purchased a home in the same county, and Curtis had something to say about it. One year later, my God sister purchased a home in the same county, and Curtis was furious at this point. Three years later, my Father left his wife and moved in with my God sister. I remember Curtis' saying to me "we moved out here to get away from your family and here they come following us". This really hurt my feelings that Curtis would say something like this when he knew how much I loved my family and how close we were. Due to my Father's health, it meant a lot to me to have him closer to me, and he could help us with the kids. With our daughter being in elementary school, Curtis and I wouldn't get off in time to get her off the bus. Therefore, my Father stepped in to help us, and he got our daughter off the bus every day. He would stay at our house until Curtis got home from work. There were times that my Father would stay until I got home because he wanted to see me. As this continued, which wasn't often, Curtis had a problem with it and wanted my Father to leave once he got home. It bothered Curtis so much until he mentioned it to his Father and his Father ended up talking to me about it. More and more, I kept seeing how Curtis really wanted me to be secluded from being around my family, which made me think why Curtis didn't have a close relationship with anyone in his family. He wasn't close to any of his sisters, brothers, nieces or nephew. He only became close to his Father when I came into his life. Curtis and his Father often thanked me for bringing them together. Up until the unexpected passing of Curtis' Father, they remained having a close relationship, and I did as well. He was an amazing Father-in-law, who was always there for me.

THREE
Hurtful First Year

"Love Like You've Never Been Hurt."
-Melissa Trinchet

As I sit here trying to remember my first year of marriage, it's hard for me to put those pieces together. Prior to marrying Curtis, we had some trust issues, and we had only known each other for four months. In hindsight, I now recognize some "red flags" that were obvious before we got married. I was aware that Curtis would pull disappearing acts, hide his pager, and I knew he was involved with a girl with whom he worked with. This girl had called me to say that she and Curtis were in a relationship. When I confronted him about it, he admitted to it and said that I was the one for him. He professed that he wanted to marry me and didn't want to lose me since he was going into the military. He kept pressing the issue of wanting to get married.

At the time, I said "yes", but in the back of my mind, I didn't know what I was thinking. We were so young; I went along with Curtis' request to get married. I wanted to get married as well because I loved Curtis and didn't want to lose him when he went into the military.

Our first year overflowed with the same trust issues that I had when we first met. We then moved to California, where he was stationed in the Navy. I remember living there and not being happy at all. There were times I was left alone because he was always in the field. When I got pregnant with our first son, that's when I felt the happiest. I felt happy because I always wanted to have kids. I had seen the joy in my sister when she had her first child.

I felt a connection with our child as soon as I found out that I was pregnant, and nothing else mattered. A little person was growing inside of me, and it was the best feeling!

During my pregnancy, I found phone numbers of females. Curtis' roommate told me he was cheating on me, and I believed him because Curtis was acting so differently towards me. He started coming home late, and it started arguments between us. I became very suspicious that something was happening. The arguments between us escalated from excessive yelling and grew to times when Curtis would physically grab and shove me. The arguments were about my accusations of him cheating and coming home late. He would not answer my calls, and I would become very upset.

I started to question myself about continuing to stay in the marriage. As I continued to be unhappy and feeling lonely, I told Curtis that I wanted to move back home. He didn't like this at all, but it was something that I needed to do since things between Curtis and I were not going well. I moved back home with my parents, which was challenging. I made my final decision because I was tired of being alone while Curtis was in the field. He wasn't happy about it, but he understood and said he would come home on the weekends to see me as often as he could. I was happy to be at home, but I was also missing Curtis. The times that Curtis was home, we had some enjoyable times watching movies, lying in the bed together, talking and hanging out with our friends.

Curtis was a Healthcare Specialist in the Navy, which was equivalent to a nurse. His position affected our relationship, because he started to have an affair with one of his co-workers. There was one evening I called Curtis when he was in California, and a woman answered his phone. My heart dropped! As I was having a conversation with this woman, the phone suddenly went silent, and when I tried to call back, the phone had been turned off. I then paged Curtis repeatedly, but I never received a call back from him until later that night. When he finally called, I asked him about the woman that answered his phone, and he said it was the police. He said he had gotten pulled over, and the police took his belongings, including his phone. I already knew that he was lying, and the feeling in my gut confirmed my suspicion. I can't remember how I got in touch with Shyanne the next day, but we ended up talking, and she told me everything. While sitting there on the phone listening to her telling me about their affair, I was rubbing my stomach. I was feeling so hurt and in disbelief that Curtis would do this to me. Why would he put me and his unborn son through this? I was beyond devastated! Shyanne said the reason why Curtis would come home late, on many nights, was because he was at her house. She also said that she had been in our house, and they had had sex in our bed. When she mentioned the sonogram picture that was on our nightstand, I was devastated to hear that Curtis had told her that I had lost the baby. I was seven months pregnant with our child at the time.

Of course, when I confronted Curtis about what Shyanne told me, he denied every bit of it. What Curtis didn't know was that Shyanne was sending me letters that he had written her while he was out in the field. I waited for a week or two, and I got a package in the mail containing all of the letters Curtis had written to Shyanne. I clearly knew his handwriting; therefore, he couldn't deny it. I felt extremely disgusted and betrayed after reading each letter. I cried profusely while reading the letters because he would say the same thing to both of us. He told her how much he loved her, how much he wanted to be with her, how he wanted to marry her, and how he wanted to have a family with her. I was so hurt, but I was trying not to get so upset because I was pregnant. I couldn't help it: I couldn't eat or sleep.

I laid in bed and secluded myself from my family and friends with my door closed shut. My family knew what was going on because I told them, and they were very upset and disappointed in Curtis. Curtis kept calling me, but I wouldn't talk to him at all. I had nothing to say to him. I just needed a break from the whole situation to figure out exactly what I wanted to do. A week went by without talking to Curtis, and I finally gave in and spoke to him when he called. He asked me why I was avoiding him, and I told him about the letters Shyanne had sent me. He vehemently denied it by saying that it wasn't his handwriting. I knew he was telling a "stupid ass" lie because I knew his handwriting. We continued to argue about this over the phone, and then he finally admitted to having an affair with her. Hearing Curtis tell me the truth crushed me even more. All I could think about was how and why my husband would do this to me. I was sad and depressed during the remaining months of my pregnancy. After numerous phone conversations, Curtis kept begging me to take him back. He said how sorry he was and that he would never do it again. So what did I do? I took Curtis back. He manipulated me so much with his words that it was almost a "curse" he put on me. I know that might sound strange to say, but he was very manipulative with his words. He really had me convinced that he would change. He had a way of making me feel guilty if I left him. Being back together wasn't the happiest feeling because I continued to stay with my parents, and Curtis stayed in California for work. The long-distance relationship was tough due to the trust issues I had, but I gave it my all. Curtis barely put any effort into the relationship. There were times when he wouldn't call me or answer my calls. His roommate told me how he would stay out and not come home some nights. He continued to come home on the weekends, and when he was home, things on the surface were good. As time was approaching for the baby's arrival, my weekly visits to the doctor's office began. Not having Curtis around to join me at my doctor's appointments made me sad, but I knew there wasn't anything I could do about it. Moving back to California wasn't an option for me.

At the beginning of my ninth month, I received a call from Shyanne, and she told me that Curtis was in jail. He had punched her in the face and attacked the man that was with her while they were sitting at a traffic light. As I was sitting on the phone listening to Shyanne crying, I couldn't believe what I was hearing. For a second, I thought she was playing a joke on me. She proceeded to tell me how Curtis had gotten upset when he saw her in the truck with a guy, and how he had come to her side of the window and punched her in the face. The guy got out to confront Curtis, and that's when they started fighting in the middle of the street. The police were called, and Curtis was taken to jail. The next day, I received a call from Curtis saying how he was set up by Shyanne and some guy and how this situation was going to cause him to be put out of the Navy. I continued to listen to his side of the story and wanted to be a supportive wife and stand by his side. However, there were witnesses who saw what happened and gave their statements to the police. These statements were shared with me by Shyanne, as she was trying to prove to me that she wasn't lying.

Yes, I will admit that I was in denial. I did not want to believe the truth about such terrible behavior by my husband, but after the investigation was done by the police and Navy officials, I had no choice but to believe it. Once the truth came full circle, Curtis couldn't deny it anymore. Having to deal with something like this while being nine months pregnant was my worst nightmare. At first, Curtis told me that he was set up, then he changed his story by saying the guy and his friend had approached him and tried to jump him at the traffic light. Curtis kept telling more lies that I didn't care to hear. I had already read the police reports and spoken with Curtis' Navy supervisor; therefore, I knew the truth. After this incident, I cut off my communication with Shyanne because I didn't need any more stress with my due date approaching. I told her that I couldn't talk to her anymore, and she respected my decision and wished me luck with my pregnancy.

After the investigation was over, it was determined, based on the evidence and statements, that Curtis was more than likely going to be dishonorably discharged from the Navy. Curtis' supervisor told him what was decided and that there would be a hearing, followed by a letter outlining the outcome. I was devastated as this was our source of income. I was nine months pregnant with the possibility of having no health insurance. What was I going to do? This unexpected, undeserved situation put me in a state of panic. All of this was going on while I was back home and while Curtis was still in California. He wasn't allowed to leave the state while his case was under investigation. I felt lost with so much disappointment in Curtis. I was embarrassed to tell my family, but I couldn't keep it from them. I knew that they would question why Curtis was home for good. I cried everyday, and I started losing weight. My doctor told me that I was allowing the stress to take a toll on me, which wasn't good for me or the baby. I had a talk with myself, and I found the inner strength to "snap" out of it. It wasn't worth risking the health of my baby for whom I needed to be strong.

As you can see, my first year of marriage was full of sadness, hurt, disappointment, infidelity, lies, abuse and drama. Why didn't I leave after the first year? What else could possibly happen after such a tumultuous year that was filled with all the warning signs? I could not answer those questions while experiencing such heartbreak. I was carrying Curtis' child, and I felt extremely confused. I blamed his cheating on me being fat and pregnant. I even questioned my self worth and concluded that I wasn't good enough for him. I didn't want to leave Curtis because we were going to have a child together. I thought that having his baby would make things better between us. I continued to have hope, and I loved this man so much that I didn't want to leave. I kept saying to myself that it will get better.

At the age of nineteen, I questioned why I was in this situation. Why was I tolerating it? In the back of my mind, I really had hope that he would change because I was having his son. I kept telling myself that Curtis would do right for his family. Sadly, there was nothing he could do to make it better. He made no effort to change. After each affair and the physical abuse, it seemed that there was another incident waiting to occur. I kept blaming myself for staying after each affair and each abusive incident. I often questioned if I deserved to be treated this way.

I stayed through all the disappointments and felt stuck, and hopeless. I wanted to leave Curtis, but the guilt of breaking up my family made me stay. I didn't feel strong enough to leave just yet.

As you read the next chapters, you will understand why I stayed as long as I did. It won't make sense to you at first, but in the end, you will have a clear sense of why. It will also give you a sense of why it's not healthy to stay in a toxic relationship. I lost myself as a woman and devoted twenty-three years of my life to a man who wasn't worthy of me, or my heart of gold. As much as I wanted to leave, I kept fighting and ignored all the signs. I delayed leaving because I was in denial and could not accept what I knew was best for me and my children. I learned that when it's time to make a change in your life, you shouldn't hesitate. When it's time to let go, it's your time to close that chapter of your life. The most important message to take away is to learn from your mistakes and your decisions. Sometimes our decisions might seem right at that moment, but those decisions can hurt us in the long run. My decision to stay as long as

I did hurt me, and I was filled with so much regret. It also hurt my children. I lost myself in loving Curtis to the point of being blinded by his controlling and manipulating ways. I forgot to love myself first. By the grace of God, we can gain wings and fly away with our dreams. We can either be the victims of our lives, or we can be the VICTORS of our lives!

FOUR
Depressed While Expecting

> *"Sometimes the person you
> love doesn't deserve you."*
> -Melissa Trinchet

After finding out about Curtis' affair with Shyanne, I forgave him and wanted to focus on moving forward. The arrival of our son was approaching, and I wanted it to be a happy experience for both Curtis and I. I was convinced that having his child would change him, and we could move on from the affair as a happy family. In the back of my mind, I kept holding on to the anger and hurt from the affair. Getting over my feelings of deception and betrayal was challenging for me; I had been deeply hurt by Curtis.

When it was time for me to go to the hospital, my contractions were starting to get unbearable. My Mother and sister didn't want me to call Curtis to tell him that I was in labor. They were both very upset with him for what he had done to me with the affair. Instead of calling Curtis to let him know, I ended up calling his cousin Faith, and I told her. She called Curtis to let him know the news. As I was being pushed into the delivery room, all I could think about was how much I wanted Curtis there to see the birth of his son. But at the same time, I didn't want him there because I was still hurt and angry with him.

I delivered our son with my mother and sister in the delivery room. When I pushed my son out, I saw that he was blue and the umbilical cord was wrapped tightly around his neck. The doctors rushed my son away as I kept screaming, "What is wrong with my baby?" After a few minutes, they brought my son back to me. The staff had to perform some immediate procedures on my son because he wasn't breathing. They told me that every safety precaution had been taken to ensure that my son was okay. As I held my son in my arms, I had a feeling I had never felt before. It was the happiest moment of my life, and I was overjoyed with tears of excitement! Curtis ended up leaving California on a "special family accommodation emergency", and he came straight to the hospital. He arrived after our son was born, but he stayed at the hospital with me all day until visiting hours were over.

When I was released from the hospital, my parents wouldn't let Curtis stay with me at their house. We had to stay with his sister who was a great help to me, with the baby. She taught me how to take care of our son. Curtis and I stayed with his sister for a week, and then he had to return to California. He was still under investigation for the domestic violence charges. When Curtis went back to California, I was allowed to go back to my parents' house. Curtis and I communicated a lot everyday, and he would tell me how much the baby had changed his life to be a better husband. He promised never to hurt me again. He repeatedly told me how important family was to him and how much he realized what he had. He promised that he would never do anything to jeopardize losing us again. The more Curtis kept saying those comforting words to me, the more I believed that we could get past the affair and start fresh. Once the investigation was done, Curtis was found guilty, and dismissed from the Navy. He came home and moved in with his grandmother.

During this time, things between Curtis and I were going okay. I ended up moving in with him at his grandmother's house since my parents still wouldn't allow Curtis in their home. Shortly after moving in, I found out about another affair that Curtis was having with a woman named Monica. This was someone he met at a nightclub, and I can't remember how I found out about the affair, but it surfaced. When I found out, I packed up my son and our things and moved back to my parents' house. I found myself feeling disappointed, hurt and betrayed again. I remember questioning myself and wondering why wasn't I good enough for him? Why did he keep having these affairs? When I confronted Curtis about it, he said that it would never happen again. He blamed it on him not thinking, and he said that Monica pursued him. Curtis also said that Monica didn't mean anything to him. He begged me over and over to forgive him, to take him back, and not to leave him. He even told me he needed his family, and just like before, I took him back. What have I done this time?

I took Curtis back, but we lived separately this time. I didn't want to move back to his grandmother's house. Although it was tough living apart, I knew that living apart for a while was the best arrangement for us. This living situation did not allow Curtis an opportunity to bond with our son and develop a relationship. There was a lot going through my mind. I felt lost while trying to understand why Curtis cheated on me for the second time. I needed time away from him; I needed time to wrap this around my head, and time to figure out what I really wanted to do. I had to decide if I wanted to work things out or divorce him. The time apart made me think about what I really wanted. Even so, Curtis wasn't giving me the time and space I needed. He would call me all the time. With my emotions all over the place, I really didn't know what I wanted. I had Curtis in one ear, my family in the other ear, and my heart was undecided. Finally, he convinced me to stay with him by saying he was sorry and that he would never do it again. I knew that I wanted my family together, and I felt like Curtis was all I knew. I didn't want to raise our son without being together. I loved this man so much; I couldn't see my life without him. I looked past the two affairs and the hurt; I sacrificed my happiness just because I felt like I couldn't move on without Curtis. His words of manipulation were working, and I basically chose to stay because that's how badly I wanted my family.

My blame cycle started over as I began to blame myself for Curtis' behavior. I questioned if I were pretty enough. Maybe, he cheated on me because I was unattractive when I was pregnant. After I had our son, I lost the weight right away. I was back to the weight I was before I got pregnant. As I continued to try to figure out what led him to cheat on me, the more I believed that it was my fault. I started to question my looks, and even the way I wore my hair and the clothes I wore. He rarely gave me compliments which was another reason why I never felt beautiful. I was so focused on pleasing him in the bed, and looking nice everyday because I thought that would stop him from having affairs, but it didn't. I did everything to please Curtis, but it was never enough. I have come to realize over the years, that it wasn't me, it was Curtis. He was the one who was insecure. He didn't value or appreciate me at all. It was clear that he needed the extra attention beyond what his wife was giving him.

FIVE
What was I Thinking?

*"No one has the right to judge the
pain inside of your heart."*
-Melissa Trinchet

I didn't leave, even though I knew that I should have. I continued to remain in a marriage that was not in my best interest. I was tired, and weary, but nothing brought me back to life and gave me hope like the face of my newborn son. He had not asked to be here, and I was not going to let him down by tearing our family apart.

Staying married to Curtis for the sake of our son was bittersweet to say the least. I remained married for seven years, had our second son and filed for a divorce in September, 2001. I was convinced that I was done with Curtis. That didn't last, as Curtis and I got back together in October, 2001, and I ended up pregnant with our daughter. We moved back in with each other and remained divorced for eleven years, before we got remarried in March of 2012. Crazy right? I agree, but again,

I wouldn't let the hope and prayers stop me from working on my marriage while trying to keep my family together. Family has always been very important to me.

I didn't realize that one day I would be repeating the cycle of what my Mother had gone through with my Father. When I was twenty-two years old, I soon learned. I believed that it was normal behavior as my Mother made it seem by continuing to stay. I remember thinking about my marriage vows, "for better, for worse," which made me want to continue to fight for my marriage.

I was raising our son back at home while Curtis was away in the military. Our arguments didn't stop, and the accusations of cheating were taking place on each end of the phone. His affair with Shyanne wouldn't leave my daily thoughts. When Curtis was finally released from the military, we were together every day, and those days together made me feel like everything between us was good. I still wasn't happy as his wife. I remember sitting there while breastfeeding my son and wondering why this man treated me the way that he did. I thought of ways that I could be a better wife, while simultaneously thinking that it wasn't me that was the problem. It was Curtis. Why wasn't I good enough for him? It remains a question that will never be answered.

The first year of raising our son was a struggle. My parents weren't happy about me being back with Curtis after all that he had put me through mentally and physically. My parents gave me an ultimatum which was to leave Curtis. If I did, I could stay home. If I didn't leave Curtis, I would have to move. I chose to stay with Curtis, and I moved out with our son to Curtis' grandmother's house.

We stayed there for a month or two, until we moved into our own apartment. Less than a month after moving, the arguments started. The arguments were because of Curtis not answering his phone when I called him. His pattern of coming home late became a concern. Due to his past affairs, I didn't trust him. I felt like something was going on and that there was another woman. One argument we had led to him being physical with me.

That same day, I confided in my sister, and I told her about the series of events. She came over when Curtis left for work. The first thing that my sister saw, when I opened the door, was my eye that was bruised, swollen and blackened. My sister couldn't believe what she saw, and she reacted strongly by crying and being very upset. "You need to leave him", she urged. Her thought was that it was only going to get worse. I told her not to tell my parents, but she did not listen. When my parents found out, my Mother took me to the police station to file for a protective order. My parents forced me to move back in with them. I didn't want to leave Curtis because I felt sorry for him, but my parents insisted.

After all that had happened, I was still attached to Curtis, even though we lived separately. When our son turned two, I got pregnant with our second son. This pregnancy was stressful due to the past indiscretions. By this time, my parents were able to look past what Curtis had done to me and agreed to him moving in with us to be with me during my pregnancy. My parents knew how important family was to me, and I convinced them that Curtis was a changed man. That was a lie! I had found out about an affair that he was having during my first trimester with a woman named Megan. I looked passed it and forgave Curtis because I wanted my family.

When our second son was born, the affair I thought he had ended with Megan was still ongoing. She had reached out to me and asked to meet up with me in person. I agreed to do so. She was very nice and spilled the beans on everything that had transpired between her and Curtis. Her story matched all the lies that Curtis had told me. As Megan and I sat there talking, she called Curtis at work. He didn't know that I was with her. They talked about what they did the night before and what their plans were going to be that evening.

That's when she said, "guess who I'm sitting with at lunch"? He asked who? She replied "your wife."

Curtis hung up on Megan and immediately called me to demand that I leave the restaurant. He advised me not to believe anything she was telling me. I believed everything Megan told me as my gut was telling me she wasn't lying. Megan was so hurt that she cried as we sat together. It was obvious to me that she really loved Curtis and believed they were going to be together.

The night I had our second son. I remember sitting in the hospital on my bed, and Curtis and I got into an argument because he didn't want to stay long at the hospital with me and the baby. It turned out that he was rushing to get back to Megan. I remember crying and not understanding why he didn't want to stay with me and our newborn son. He grabbed me by my nose and told me he was sick of the bullshit and that he had to get home so he could get up early for work.

I learned that my brother knew about the affair Curtis was having with Megan. Because he didn't want to get in the middle of it, my brother chose not to tell me. After finding this out, I felt betrayed by my brother, but I also understood his position.

Eventually, Curtis admitted to the affair he was having with Megan. I no longer knew what to think or feel. When nothing changes, nothing changes. I started to feel like I was the only one who was in the dark.

SIX
The Affairs

"Internal pain and tears can tell a story."
-Melissa Trinchet

Soon after we got married, we started to have issues with a woman named Debbie who said that she and Curtis were in a relationship prior to the time when Curtis and I started to date. When I confronted Curtis about what Debbie had told me, he denied it. After several arguments and me telling Curtis that I wanted to end things with him, he finally admitted to it. He immediately ended things with Debbie, and we had no more issues with her. We proceeded to work on our marriage. In June, 1994, I became pregnant with our first child, and I moved to California to be with Curtis since he was stationed there in the Navy. The first evidence of an affair was when I found phone numbers stuffed behind an ashtray in his car. He told me that they were nothing, and he threw them out of the window. During my short time in California, the physical abuse started. Curtis shoved and grabbed me when we would have arguments. As this progressed, I decided to move back home to be with my family to give us a break.

Soon after I returned home, I found out about his first actual affair with a woman named Sheyanne who also was in the Navy. I ended up speaking to Sheyanne because she answered his cell phone one day when I called Curtis, and she questioned who I was. As we talked on the phone, she told me how Curtis told her that he was going through a divorce. She then asked me about a sonogram picture that was in his room. I told her that it was a picture of our son. I also told her that I was seven months pregnant, and she said in a shocked voice, "You're pregnant"? "He told me the sonogram was of his son and that you had lost the baby".

This is when I ended things with Curtis, and he continued to have his affair with Sheyanne. A week later, he begged me to take him back because he wanted his family back and that he would never cheat on me again.

As we were working on our marriage, I found out about another affair he had had with a woman named Monica. He had met Monica at a nightclub. When I confronted him about the affair, he denied it, until I confronted him with the woman. We were all face to face which made it impossible for Curtis to deny his involvement. Again, he apologized and said it would never happen again, and I took him back.

Our second son was born, and during this pregnancy, Curtis was caught again cheating with another woman named Megan. This affair went on for a while before I found out by meeting up with the woman. We had Curtis on a three-way call, and again, he apologized and asked me to forgive him. At this point I needed to talk to someone that was close to Curtis about his repeated affairs. Since I had become very close to his Father, I had to speak with him about Curtis' affairs. His Father became very upset as he had heard of the other women; however, he never talked to Curtis about them.

He asked Curtis and I to come to his house so that he could talk to us. He told me, in front of Curtis, that I deserved to leave him and to not give Curtis another chance. As we were all sitting there, Curtis started crying while asking me to give him another chance. He reacted the same way by promising he wouldn't hurt me again.

So what did I do? I took Curtis back. A couple of years went by, and at this point, my trust for him was slowly going downhill. I found out about another work affair he was having with a woman named Sherry. I remember feeling so drained emotionally. I cried every day while trying to understand how this man could put me through this again while I was carrying our second son. The affair with Sherry was so messy! This woman would call and tell me all this stuff about her and Curtis, and mind you, I was towards the end of my pregnancy! At this point, I was so devastated with having to go through the drama with Curtis' affair with Megan, I now had to deal with another one. Sherry somehow got my email address and was sending me emails, and she would call my phone saying mean things to me. I ended up talking to Sherry, and she said Curtis told her we weren't together anymore. He had told another lie and had deceived me and another woman because he and I were living together as a married couple. Again, he apologized and asked me to forgive him.

I finally found the strength to convince myself that I had had enough. I said enough was enough, and I divorced Curtis in September of 2001. That following month, he asked me to take him back, and I did. That's when I got pregnant with our daughter. Curtis ended up leaving the contracting company, and he returned to the prior contracting company he had worked for when he was released from the Navy. I was also working at the same place, and during his time of working in the same building, Curtis ended up having another work affair with a woman named Allison. She was an investigator on his floor, and their affair lasted a few months until I found out by confronting both of them. The affair ended, and I took him back as he begged me not to leave him. A few months went by and Curtis was promoted to a manager's position at a different location with another contracting company.

You guessed it; he ended up having another work affair with a married woman named Mary. I remember standing at our bedroom door asking God to send me a sign about Curtis and his cheating. My gut kept telling me that he was up to no good. As I stood there, I felt a push telling me to go in his closet and to put my hands through his shirts. That's when I found a cellphone. I believed that this was God telling me that I had more than enough evidence to leave Curtis. Prior to this feeling, I had gone to church the day before, and I prayed about my situation with Curtis. I truly felt that God had heard my prayer, and I knew this sign was God answering my prayers.

I confronted both of them about the secret cell phone, and they both denied it until I provided them, including Mary's husband, with a copy of the phone bill. I decided that I was going to pack my stuff and leave, but Curtis begged me not to leave as he stood at my closet door with a pitiful look on his face.

I ignored the sign from God and stayed because I loved Curtis and didn't want to hurt my kids.

After this affair, things settled down, and each day our marriage started to slowly improve for the better. Curtis and I were getting along, and he was a totally different person. In 2010, I planned a dinner with our friends and both of our families. I surprised Curtis by asking him to re-marry me. The abuse and the affairs had stopped, and I was actually rebuilding my trust for Curtis. A year later, Curtis told me to start looking for venues so we could have a nice, beautiful wedding. The planning started, and I was so excited about it! We got remarried, which was the happiest moment of my life. It was a very happy time, not just for us, but for our children, family and friends to witness this beautiful, special moment. This made me believe that this time around, we could actually survive the storm and put the past behind us and begin a fresh start.

In May of 2012, Curtis went to Memphis, TN for a five day manager's course that was required for managers/supervisors to attend. This course was important to Curtis because he was receiving a certificate of completion for taking the course. One day while Curtis was already in Memphis, I was talking to one of our mutual co-workers who has a high ranked position in the government, and he asked me why I didn't go to support Curtis. He went on saying how he takes his wife with him to conferences and training courses. As I am sitting there thinking about what he's saying, the more it made me feel like "shit" because Curtis never asked me to go out of town with him. I responded and said, "I would love to support Curtis, but I never get asked to go with him". He then proceeded to say, "well, you know he's getting a certificate for completing this important manager course, and you should surprise him and attend the ceremony". I immediately thought is was a great idea! Therefore, he helped me plan my flight and contacted the agency who was hosting the course to have me picked up from the airport, and I contacted the hotel. Everything was set, and Curtis knew nothing about the surprise. I was so happy to be able to be there for him as I knew how important this was to Curtis, prior to him leaving for Memphis. I got picked up from the airport; I arrived at the hotel, and they had my hotel room key waiting for me. I went to Curtis' room. At the time I arrived, he was still in class, so the surprise was going great as planned. When I got to the room, I showered and put on a sexy lingerie, and I laid in the bed. When Curtis arrived, he would see me in the bed looking sexy for him. When he finally opened the door, he was shocked and said while smiling, "what are you doing here", I replied, "I wanted to surprise you and be here for the ceremony when you receive your certificate". He said, "this is a great surprise, thank you!" Curtis got undressed, and he laid in the bed with me, kissing on me, and we had a great time! We stayed in bed talking, cuddling and watching TV until it was time to start getting ready for the banquet ceremony. We took a shower together as we usually do and got dressed. The night was going great! Curtis received his certificate, and he introduced me to his team. We danced and then we sat down to talk to some colleagues we knew. As I am sitting there directly in front of Curtis, an Asian woman comes behind Curtis as he's sitting down and puts her arms around him and leans her face into his ear to where her head was laying sideways on his shoulder. Here I am, Curtis' wife watching this "shit" go down while Curtis doesn't budge at all to remove her hands from around him or bother to get up. Instead, he continued to sit there and do absolutely nothing! I couldn't hear what she was saying to him because she was so close to his ear and there was music playing. At this point I couldn't believe what I was seeing. I was heated and felt so disrespected not just by her, but by my husband! When she finally decided to remove herself and walk away, she looked at me with a smirk, and as I got up to approach her, Curtis grabbed me, and we left the banquet to go back to the room. When we got in the room, I asked him what she said to him, and he said it was nothing, she was drunk. He was lying to me; I knew my gut was telling me that something was going on between them. I started packing my stuff and told him I was going home. Curtis asked me why I was leaving, and I said "you can't be serious, your ass just had a woman disrespect me while you sat there and did nothing"!!! As I kept packing my stuff, Curtis kept grabbing on me telling me it was nothing and for me not to leave. At this point I was so hurt with my eyes filled with tears. The argument started to get worse with both of us yelling, and Curtis put his hand around my mouth, told me to shut up and threw me on the bed. He insisted that I wasn't going anywhere and that I was overreacting. Overreacting my ass! I then said to Curtis, "If a man did that to me in your face, you would go off, so don't play this game with me". He begged me not to leave, and we ended up falling asleep. I laid there in tears as Curtis wouldn't remove his arms from around me. The next morning, it was time to catch the shuttle to the airport, and I had no words for Curtis. I just wanted to get back home to my kids. He kept trying to make small talk with me, and I told him it's best that he just be quiet and leave me the hell alone. As we were on the shuttle bus driving to the airport, all I could think about was "here we go again, back to square one of being disrespected by Curtis involving another female." Mind you, Curtis and I were in our second month of being re-married!

In February, 2013, eleven months after being remarried, another work affair surfaced. Her name was Elizabeth, and she knew he was married and knew about me. I found out about this affair by getting in his email account. As I kept scrolling down reading the back and forth emails between Curtis and Elizabeth, I was so hurt and couldn't believe what Curtis was saying to her. He was telling her that she looked gorgeous and how he would enjoy giving her massages.

Curtis rarely complimented me on my looks nor had he ever offered to give me a massage. I used to beg him to give me a massage! Another thing that blew my mind about this affair was his reply when I asked him why he did it. He said he didn't know and that it was all talk. He continued to tell me that the "peck" kiss on her lips was just a "good luck" kiss because she was leaving for another job. He then said to me how I should have never read his emails. As much as I wanted to slap him for making that heartless comment to me, all I could do was cry. At this point, my trust was completely gone, and my heart was shattered into a million pieces. I had faced extreme disappointment after each broken promise. I could no longer stay at work, and I went to my supervisor's office and cried in her arms as she consoled me. She let me go home, but before I left, I forwarded the email to Curtis and Elizabeth to let them know that I was fully aware of their affair.

When I left work, I called my Father-in-law in tears. I was so emotional, and I couldn't say what I wanted to tell him. My heart was completely crushed, and I couldn't believe that after being remarried for the second time that Curtis would do this to me and our kids again. As I calmed down to tell his Father, he was so disappointed in Curtis and couldn't believe it. He said, "Lisa, I know that's my son, but you need to really leave him this time". He also said "enough is enough, Curtis doesn't deserve you". He kept apologizing for Curtis' actions as he tried to comfort me over the phone.

After speaking to my Father-in-law, I called my friend, Katie, who only knew half of what I had been through with Curtis. I was crying on the phone and told her what had just happened. She knew how hurt I was and told me to meet her at Fridays so we could talk. As I was getting out of the car, somehow, Curtis knew I was there and pulled up to the restaurant and demanded me to leave to go home so he and I could talk. I told him "no" and that I had nothing to say to him. At that time, my friend Katie got out of her car, and he told her to leave. I begged Katie not to leave and to stay with me. Katie saw the hurt and scared look on my face, and she came over to my car and we walked into the restaurant. Curtis was not happy about this at all, and he ended up pulling off. When I got home, he followed me upstairs to our bedroom and kept asking me to please talk to him. He kept begging me to stay and to not leave him. Yes, I ended up staying, but this time I had a plan.

At this point, I knew in my heart that I was done and no longer in love with Curtis. I started to think of ways to leave Curtis. I struggled after each affair with trying to trust him so many times. The realization that Curtis, the accuser, played a huge part in our failed marriage had to be faced. I stayed as long as I did because I didn't want to break up my family, Curtis was all I knew, and I kept hoping and praying that he would change after each promise.

The last and final affair in 2016 was another reason why I knew in my heart that it was time for me to leave Curtis. This work affair was with a married women named Susan who lived near our house and who Curtis was secretly giving rides to work. He changed his work hours so that they would both arrive at work extra early before the other employees arrived. What he didn't know was I had his code to his work phone and saw calls between them after work hours as well as text messages. There was one day he came home from work and went straight upstairs to take a shower, which was unlike him. When he went into the shower, I noticed how strangely he was acting. This made me pay attention to the color underwear he was wearing. I had a suspicion that he had done something.

That next day when I went to do the laundry, I noticed that the underwear he had worn the day before weren't in the hamper. When I asked him about them, he said he put them in there and that I must have done something with them to start an argument. I knew exactly what he had done with them. He had thrown them away as he was clearly hiding something. The signs of his affair with Susan continued. They were meeting up in the evenings. One time I saw them both leaving the area of one of our shopping center. He was also leaving the house in the evenings and not saying where he was going. Of course, Curtis denied this affair, and at this point, I didn't care anymore. I didn't have the energy to show the proof as I was already checked out from the marriage. I had decided to leave Curtis.

The time and effort Curtis put into having each of these affairs took away the attention my husband was lacking in giving me. I had been asking him to show me some love and attention for years. As much as I wanted to step out to get the attention I was missing from him, the love I had for this man wouldn't allow me to do so. He didn't think about me or the kids prior to having each affair. He didn't think about the consequences it would have as he clearly didn't care. As I found out about each affair, the more I felt disrespected. For twenty-three years, Curtis never cared to put me and our children first. Instead, he chose to hurt us with his countless affairs, and he chose to physically abuse me.

I was no longer going to let this man have his 9th affair or allow him to put his hands on me again while hurting the kids at the same time.

SEVEN
Not Feeling Loved or Wanted

"Understand your worth as a person."
-Melissa Trinchet

During my twenty-three years of marriage, I can only remember a few times when I felt loved and appreciated by Curtis. One day he surprised me with a candle light dinner after a day of work. This event took place after my parents had put me out, and we lived together at his grandmother's house. Sadly, this was one of the few and only sentimental memories that has stuck with me out of all those years of being together. During the rest of my time with Curtis, I didn't feel loved or wanted by him. The only time I would hear Curtis say he loved me was when I would say it first or when he was drunk. Most of the time, I felt like I was just there for show on his arm and as the Mother of his kids.

He never wanted to do anything together as a couple, and he never wanted to do things that I wanted to do. He barely told me he loved me; he rarely gave me any nice compliments.

When I used to go up to hug him, he would barely hug me back. I always had to be the one to initiate a kiss, and his body language showed that he didn't want to be bothered with me. He didn't like going to the movies because he said it was a waste of money. I can't remember the last time we went out to eat with just him and I. If he wanted to go sit at a bar and drink, and I didn't want to go, he had a problem with it.

As for family trips, I had to plan them all, and most of the time, he complained about doing them because of money and not wanting to take time off from work. However, he planned team bonding outings with his coworkers and outings with his friends. He would miss some of our kids' sporting activities to be with his coworkers and friends. When Curtis and I would go out with friends, he always belittled me in front of them by bringing up things from the past. His demeanor was so cocky about everything. This became such a problem that our friends stopped asking us to go out with them. They didn't like his behavior towards me at all. I also noticed the decrease in invites to family and friends functions because all Curtis did was talk down to his family and our friends, and make negative comments.

The ongoing mental and physical abuse, along with the affairs, killed my self-esteem. I didn't know my worth as a woman. I always felt like I wasn't good enough for him. When I questioned Curtis about why he continued to put his hands on me, his excuse was because he saw it done to his Mother, and he thought it was normal.

I fought and fought to keep my marriage and family together, but eventually there was no more fighting left in me. I satisfied Curtis in the bedroom, and I was spontaneous. Sadly, this was the only connection we had together that we both enjoyed. I made sure to look pretty everyday, and I wore nice clothing. I kept our home cleaned, cooked and took great care of our three children. Apparently, this wasn't enough for Curtis. I felt myself struggling to keep my marriage together, but I was in it alone. Just because you love someone doesn't mean you're meant to be with them. Never let a man's inability to love you the way that you deserve convince you that you're the problem. Sometimes, they're just too cowardly to admit that it's not easy to consistently try to match your fly!

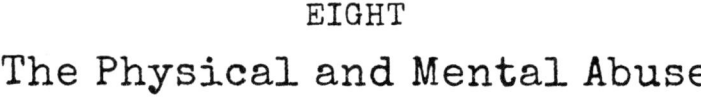

EIGHT
The Physical and Mental Abuse

*"Rebuild yourself and come back
even stronger than ever."*
-Melissa Trinchet

The first physical abuse incident was when we got into a heated argument at a family gathering at Curtis' cousin Faith's house, over his cheating. He refused to let me leave. He kept pushing me and grabbing on me. His family got involved and pulled him away, and as I was driving off he came running towards my car, and busted the front windshield with his fist. Glass shattered everywhere in the car. It was on me, and on our son who at that time was six months old. Curtis then got in his car and followed me until I pulled up to the parking lot of the fire department near his aunt's house. He blocked me in and came over to the car while yelling and demanding me to unlock the door. I did, but I was terrified and didn't know what was going to happen. I was crying and trying to calm our son who was also crying. Curtis started crying and saying that he didn't want to lose his family. He kept apologizing for what he had done.

That evening, I went home and told my parents what had happened. They were very upset, especially my Father. That same evening, my Father made me file for an emergency protection order. Following this order, Curtis and I were no longer together. A month or so later, we ended up getting back together, and we got an apartment. After moving in, we got into a violent argument. Curtis got so angry that when I tried to walk away from him he punched me in the left eye. I was holding our son in my arms when I fell to the living room floor. He hovered over me, and he started crying and apologizing. He kept saying how he didn't mean to do it. He started saying that he needed help for why he's the way he is. I remember crying and feeling so hurt with disbelief that he had put his hands on me again. The next day, I tried to use makeup to cover up the black eye, but it didn't work. I avoided my family, and I didn't go to work for a few days. However, I could no longer avoid the black eye or stay in denial of what had just happened. I went back to work while feeling insecure, and embarrassed about the way I looked with a bruised eye.

When I had to face my family, they were outraged. My mother took me to the police station and informed the officer that I already had a protection order in place against Curtis. Charges were filed, and he was found guilty for violating the protection order and was sentenced to six months in jail. He ended up serving four months for good behavior. During his time of being incarcerated, he called me repeatedly with apologies, and he begged me to come see him. He told me that he wanted to see me and his son. I ended up giving in and went to visit him a few times. Each time I went to visit Curtis, he begged me to take him back, and he kept apologizing.

When he came home from jail, we ended up seeing each other again, but we lived separately because we continued to argue. A month went by, and we ended up seeing each other at a party. When Curtis saw me, he tried to talk to me. I walked away, and that's when he grabbed me, and we started fighting because he wouldn't let me go. The police were called, and Curtis ran off and left the party. The abuse continued throughout the years with him pushing me, shoving me, poking me, slapping me, choking me, kicking me out of our bed, and pulling my hair. One time, he yanked me out of a limo on the night of my birthday celebration, and he dragged me on to the sidewalk in front of our family and friends. They all had to pull Curtis off me. This was a terrible, crazy night!! Another incident was when I walked out of our bedroom in the middle of our arguing to walk in the kitchen, and he yelled at me, telling me to stop walking away from him. That's when Curtis pushed me from the back, and I hit my head on the kitchen counter and busted my head. I was bleeding, and I yelled into the living room and told his niece to call the police. She just sat there on the couch and didn't do anything to help. Curtis grabbed me and began pleading, saying he didn't mean for it to happen. He kept apologizing. When I looked at my head, there was a long gash that wouldn't stop bleeding. Curtis stayed there with me the entire time, applying pressure to stop the bleeding. Since the bleeding wouldn't stop, I had to go to the hospital to get four stitches. When the nurse asked me what happened, I told her I tripped over someone's foot and hit the kitchen counter. I now have a scar on the front left side of my head that's noticeable due to my hair not growing back.

There was another incident when he yanked me by my hair when we were arguing upstairs in our bedroom. My Father and daughter were downstairs. I tried to leave the house, and he slammed my face in the door. However, I was still able to run out. When my oldest son came home, he knew something was wrong because he saw his sister crying, and my Father had told him what had happened. My son left the house to find me to make sure I was okay. He asked me what happened, and I told him.

In April, 2013, two months after I had found out about his affair with Elizabeth, I told him that I was invited by one of my best friends to go to New York to celebrate her birthday. He told me I wasn't allowed to go. I asked him why, and he said, "married women don't go on trips with single women, and you're staying home." I told him that the trip was already paid for, and that I was going. He said, "If you go, consider us over." My response was "okay." We fought everyday about the trip until the day I left.

February, 2016, I was getting dressed to go out, and as I was putting on my makeup in the living room bathroom, Curtis asked me where I was going? I told him that it was none of his business, since he comes and goes as he pleases. I tried to close the bathroom door, and he pushed on the door so hard that the top door hinge cracked. He then forced his way back in and slapped my eyeshadow case out of my hand. He grabbed me by my neck, pushed me against the wall, and told me that I'd better watch who I was talking to. He stated that I needed to respect him. He had his hand pressed so tightly around my neck until I started to have problems breathing. I then dug my nails into his hand to get him to stop choking me. Once he released his hand, I left the bathroom, and he pushed me onto the living room chair. He started poking me in my face and chest and telling me how I wasn't shit. He told me that nobody was going to want me with three kids and that I was fat. As I tried to leave the house, he kept pushing me, and telling me that I wasn't going anywhere. I tried to leave again, and he tried to stop me. I screamed as loud as I could, and he finally let me leave.

On May 2, 2016 Curtis asked me to come downstairs. He said that he wanted to show me something. I refused several times, and that's when he warned me that I'd better come downstairs. When I walked into my oldest son's room, he poked his finger in my face with anger in his voice and told me I'd better change my profile picture on my Instagram page. The picture was a faraway picture of me in a bathing suit. When I moved his hand from my face, he pushed me hard on my chest on to my son's bed. He called me all types of mean names and told me to pack my stuff and get out. He said he also found out that I had a Facebook account, and he called me an attention seeking whore. When I proceeded to go back upstairs, he pushed me down a couple stairs, but I continued to go upstairs. When we got to the second set of stairs, he grabbed me by my arm and told me to get out of his house. When I finally got to our room to go to my closet, I told him that I was going to my dad's house. He tried to close the closet door on me, and he pushed me again. He kept saying that if I left, he would get me for abandonment, even though he was the one that told me to get out. That's when I grabbed my pillows and went downstairs to go to my son's room. Curtis followed me downstairs and pushed me on the bed. He tackled me and took my cell phone. He continued to say mean things to me, and finally he left the room.

July 25, 2016, was the first day of my job working at an institute where I had previously worked. I arrived on campus, and as I was getting ready to park, my gut told me to drive down to the lower level of the garage to see where Curtis had parked. I had suspicious thoughts of him meeting up with the married woman, Susan, at work. As I proceeded to drive down to the lower level of the garage, my gut kept telling me to keep going. That's when I saw Curtis' truck parked next to Susan's car. Their cars were the only two cars there. The crazy part about this incident is that Curtis appeared out of nowhere. As he came around the corner, he was sweating, and he looked at me with so much anger in his eyes. He began asking me what I was doing. The look on his face told it all. He was shocked with guilt and caught in the middle of what I already knew was happening. As I pulled off, Curtis reached his arm in the car, and he punched me in my chin. I went to park on the upper level of the garage, and cried. I tried to stop crying, knowing that I had to get myself together for my first day of work.

December 18, 2016, it had now been a month and a half after I left Curtis, and moved out. I began receiving calls from Curtis at 2:00 am, followed by a knock on my door. I thought something was wrong, so I let him in. When he came into the house, he stood at the bottom of the steps by the front door. As he came closer, I could smell the alcohol on him. He started going off on me, yelling and poking his finger in my face. He poked me so hard in my forehead and said how he didn't appreciate the fact that my friend Joyce was giving our daughter advice. I didn't know where this was coming from. Joyce hadn't done anything wrong in talking to our daughter about how to make friends. The angry rage in Curtis' eyes made me afraid. I was too scared to say anything to him. I didn't want it to escalate to anything serious. He proceeded to yell at me while spitting with his words and poking his finger in my face. I asked him to please leave, but he kept yelling at me with his drunk, slurred words. I started crying and asked him again to please leave, and as he was walking out the door, he called me a fat, thirsty bitch, and slammed the door.

In addition to the physical abuse, the mental abuse was just as hurtful. He told me I was a terrible wife and Mother, and that my Mother didn't raise me right. Some of the mean things he would say to me happened during his drunk episodes at public outings, and in our home when family and friends visited. After each drunk episode when Curtis was sober, I would tell him how he had acted towards me and about the mean things he had said to me. He would promise me that he was done with drinking, and he wouldn't do it again. However, the drunk episodes continued over and over, and the verbal abuse continued as well.

NINE
The Cycles of Life

"You can accept people for who they are, but don't accept their behavior."
—Melissa Trinchet

I continued to question myself for staying with Curtis, but there were also times that my mind wandered towards Curtis, and why he was the way he was. Of course, we all have some fault in whether a relationship fails or prospers, but I couldn't help but think of the repeated affairs and abuse. When I learned about Curtis' childhood from some of his family members, his friends and from him, I started to understand why he was the way he was. Curtis was repeating the revolving cycle he had experienced as a child and as a teenager.

Curtis grew up in a very strict home with his Father and Mother until the age of seven. Curtis went to school, and he had to go straight home after school to do his homework, eat dinner, work out and go to sleep. As a child, Curtis was barely allowed to go outside to play with his friends. His Father kept him in the house working on sports. Curtis was very competitive and won a lot of sport competitions. When Curtis was almost eight, his Mother left his Father for another man. When Curtis' Mother left, he became very angry with his Father and started to be rebellious against his Father. As Curtis got older, he started to hang around the wrong crowd and kept getting in trouble. As Curtis told me, this was his way of dealing with the pain of his Mother leaving them. He blamed it all on his Father, and the way his Father treated his Mother for so many years. The issues between Curtis and his Father continued as Curtis got older. As I was told by Curtis, it all got worse when his Father married his high school counselor, who was white. Curtis had a real issue with it and felt embarrassed by it. His school friends knew, and they would talk about it. Before Curtis met me through his cousin, he wanted to confirm with her that I was not fully white. His cousin told him that I was mixed with Cuban and Puerto Rican, and he agreed to meet me. I never knew what Curtis' issue was with white women, but apparently it was an issue for him at that time.

When Curtis was younger, his family was very close and always had family gatherings at his grandmother's house. Curtis' grandmother was the glue that kept the family together. After her passing, the family started to fall apart, and the attendance to the family functions started to get smaller and smaller. Curtis' relationship with his family was off and on when he and I met. Curtis often distanced himself from his family, and he rarely wanted to go to his family functions. The only time Curtis and his family would all get together was once a year for a family, holiday gathering.

Curtis had grown up with structure and strict rules. I learned that even between Curtis' Mother and Father, there were fights, cheating and some physical abuse. Curtis estranged relationship with his Father stemmed from his anger about his Mother leaving them and his Father's new wife, who was white and his high school counselor. Curtis was also angered over the fact that his friends would laugh about it. He was often embarrassed.

Curtis blamed his Father as the reason why his Mother left. In retrospect, I believe that all that he had seen and heard led him to believe that cheating and abuse were normal. I knew better, but I just hadn't quite figured out the skills or had the strength that I needed to do better.

TEN
Facing the Lady in the Mirror

"Never doubt the person you are on the outside, brace it with happiness."
-Melissa Trinchet

Who am I? I have asked myself this question plenty of times. I started to question who I was when I felt like I wasn't good enough for Curtis. I started to feel like I wasn't pretty. I didn't like my body, and I didn't feel worthy. I would wear bathing suits and nice outfits and was told often by women and men how nice I looked, but I was in denial. In my mind, my body wasn't good enough for Curtis. I knew I had a nice curvy body, but I didn't think it was good enough. I continued to not feel sexy. I was ashamed and didn't like the bikini c-section scar I had after having two of my children. As often as I was told how beautiful I was by my kids, family, friends and even strangers, I never believed them. I loved hearing the compliments, but I could never internalize them. I was with a man for twenty three years who barely ever complimented me or paid any attention to me. I doubted myself and felt insecure about my looks.

Curtis made me feel like I wasn't good enough due to his ongoing affairs. Even though I understood the importance of how I should be feeling on the inside and realized that I had a heart of gold, I can't tell you how hard it was to wake up every morning, look in the mirror and just cry. The tears would flow like a running water faucet. I kept thinking the mirror was broken, but it was just me who was broken - I was the broken one. Every false sense of encouragement I try to feed myself shattered me into a million pieces on the bathroom floor. In the mirror, I didn't look pretty as I was convinced that I wasn't pretty at all. My self esteem had hit rock bottom; I would avoid looking at myself in the mirror. I even questioned if I should have cosmetic surgery, which shows you how weak of a woman I had become. I wasn't happy with myself at all. However, I had to get myself together and face my three children with a fake smile. It was a routine that I was too familiar with. Being pretty doesn't heal the pain. In the end, it was my soul that needed surgery.

It has taken some time for me to learn to love myself and be proud for the rest of my life. I have arrived at a time when I realize that God has blessed me with three healthy babies, and I will be forever thankful. My self esteem hit rock bottom, and it took two years before I left Curtis for me to finally realize that there was nothing wrong with my body. I began to walk around in confidence with my head held high, and I started to look in the mirror and tell myself how beautiful I am!

ELEVEN
Praying by Kesha

"Never give up on yourself, get back up,
be brave, be happy."
   -Melissa Trinchet

This song came out during the time of my healing after leaving Curtis. Talk about great timing, HA! I listened to the song over and over again. The words from the beginning to the end spoke to me, as it related to what I was going through. Being in a dark place, with thoughts of not wanting to live anymore, wasn't a good place to be at all. I felt helpless with a broken, shattered heart. I continued to pray and receive love and support from my family and friends. I listened to the song and prayed until I was able to find the strength to remove those thoughts. I was also able to recognize my worth as a strong woman. I promised myself that I would never EVER let myself get to a dark place like that again. It wasn't how terrible Curtis treated me that got me to that dark place; it was the fact that I allowed myself to get to that point. I never got an apology for what I went through. I held on for so long, waiting for Curtis to say "I apologize, and I shouldn't have done that to you." Instead, I was always told, "I don't know what you're talking about", and you're making this up in your head because that never happened." I had to pick up those pieces, and stitch them back together. My experiences traumatized me to a dark place in my life.

As I still continue to struggle with finding myself, I know I will eventually get there. I had a minor set back by allowing a man whom I met through a close friend to come into my life during my time of healing. When we met, it was "lust" at first sight. We both latched on to each other instantly, which had a lot to do with what he and I didn't get in our past relationships. As I look back at it now, I believe that we were each other's rebound. We had an understanding that we were just going to be "cool" friends and hang out and have fun - nothing serious at all. However, we instantly connected and hit it off non-stop for six months.

He had just gotten out of a four year relationship, and I was in my tenth month of being single after leaving Curtis. We were great together, and we were both happy being around each other. We shared private things with each other from our past, along with giving each other advice on how to handle certain things we both faced. In the beginning, he was everything I wanted in a man. He was affectionate, respectful, caring, supportive, and he made me happy. He treated me like a queen, and he was great with my daughter, my family and friends. Everyone liked him. I smiled often, and I could be myself around him. We could undress each other with our eyes. That's how passionate, and strong the attraction was between us. He made me feel loved, wanted and beautiful which I had never felt from Curtis.

However, when I decided to cut things off with him to protect my heart, as things started to get too serious with our feelings, he crossed that line of disrespect with his choice of words. I wasn't going to tolerate that type of behavior, and I decided to end our friendship. He was upset that I wanted to end the intimate part of our friendship which hurt me at the same time, but I had to do what was best for me. His choice of the way he lived his "triangle" personal life consisted of things that I could no longer be a part of. With that being said, his stubbornness, ego and pride were more important than saving our friendship with a simple apology. He clearly didn't value our friendship as much as I did.

When you've done something wrong, admit to it and be sorry sooner than later. No one in history has ever choked to death from swallowing their pride. If your pride is bigger than your heart and your ego is bigger than your head, grow up, or you will be alone for life! It's better to lose your pride for someone you love and/or care about, rather than lose that someone you love and/or care about with your useless pride. Sadly, it took him a month to reach out to me to finally apologize. By this time, he had shown his true colors, and I lost all respect for him as a man and as a friend. He showed me that entire month of not hearing from him that he didn't care about our friendship. I didn't look at him as that loyal friend he once was to me. After his apology, we remained friends for about two weeks. I found out that he had lied to me about some things, and he broke some promises he had made to me.

This was enough, and I no longer wanted a liar who was full of games a part of my life. He no longer deserved my loyal and genuine friendship. Therefore, I chose to cut him off for good, and I never looked back. I refused to let an immature "grown" man disrespect me and lie to me. He started to remind me of Curtis. He wasn't completely honest with me about certain things, and he knew it. As "friends," he didn't know how to be loyal or how to value a good friendship. Instead, he chose to ruin it with his immature actions. He knew what my past consisted of, and he promised me that he would never hurt me. Well, he did and in more ways than one.

His lies, games, and not being there for me coupled with his choice of disrespectful words defined his immaturity. It was sad because he damn sure put on a good front when I first met him. I was nothing but good to him as he often told me how good I treated him and how much he loved me. However, those "good treated days" ended when I reacted to his heartless actions by giving him a taste of his own medicine! Don't dish out what you can't handle when the tables are turned. Raul, you lost a great friend!

So there I was, picking up the pieces from another situation I had to end to protect my heart. I continued to find my worth as a woman. Moving forward, I know I need to focus on me, do me and get in touch with myself to make me happy first. When I give my all, I give it to the fullest, and when I love hard, I love to my core. However, I found out the hard way that I get nowhere by doing either. So today, my testimony is to say that I am no longer going to settle for bullshit! I regret nothing in my life, even if my past was full of hurt. I still look back and smile because it made me who I am today. I have learned how to let go of regret and to forgive. I will continue to keep building because better is coming as God told me so through prayer. Maturity is learning to walk away from people and situations that threaten your peace of mind, self respect, values, morals and self worth. I won't run from my issues; I will face them head on as the strong woman I am today. I'm getting stronger with every test I pass. My life is getting better every day, and my mistakes have made me wiser.

So today, I leave you with this quote, "You only put a dent in my heart; you never broke me. I just needed to re-adjust my CROWN and fearlessly step into the new me"! It's that heart of gold and stardust soul that make me BEAUTIFUL, and I am that new me, Lisa Marie. I will continue to rise above and find my inner happiness, but most importantly, I will find out who Lisa Marie is! You see, I wasn't completely broken because my "Elastic Heart" was strong enough not to snap.

As for where I am today with my friends, let's just say I had to end a few friendships due to lies, two faceted ways and back stabbing. When you're a loyal friend to someone, you expect the same in return. Well, that wasn't the case for the ones I had to cut off. The friends I chose to remove from my life was the best decision I made as I chose not to have liars in my life. Some of them took my divorce and the pain I was going through as if it were some celebrity TMZ news. When all along they weren't my friends from the beginning. They were going around gossiping about me as if their marriages/relationships were perfect! If they only knew what I know about their messy ways as well as their spouses messy ways, they wouldn't have been parading my divorce around town. The small circle of loyal friends I have today have never let me down, and they have been there for me through the ups and downs since day one. I never had to question their friendship, loyalty, love, support and honesty. They are my "ride or dies," and they know exactly who they are. I love each of you dearly!

TWELVE

Courage To Finally Leave

*"My heart has known great pain, but
finding my happiness started with healing."*
-Melissa Trinchet

September, 2016, I filed for an absolute divorce. I was still feeling unsure about leaving Curtis because I wanted to keep my family together. I knew deep down inside that it was the best decision. The weekend before he left to go out of town for a work meeting, which was October 28, 2016, we got into an argument. At this point, we were arguing everyday about me not trusting him, catching him in lies, and him leaving the house without saying anything. He continued to come home late, and his drunk episodes along with my feelings of not being loved or wanted had left me mentally drained. I finally realized that Curtis didn't value his family enough to change for the better. During this argument, I told him that I was serious about moving out since we both were in an agreement. He said he didn't want to be with me anymore due to my trust issues and assumptions. However, I asked him before I made the move of leaving him if he wanted to try marriage counseling to help with the issues in our marriage, and his immediate response was" NO." He laughed about it! He said he didn't have any issues and didn't want to talk to anybody as it would be a waste of money.

That night I remember crying myself to sleep while trying to understand why my husband of twenty three years didn't want to go to counseling to fix what was broken to save his marriage and keep our family together. I thought about all the affairs and wondered why I wasn't good enough for him. It's twenty three years later, and I'm still asking myself this same question. I couldn't understand why the kids and I weren't enough happiness for him. I struggled to find the answer to why he had to keep having the affairs that didn't just hurt me, but they also hurt our kids. They always saw their Mother who often cried and heard their parents arguing.

Curtis clearly didn't want to change or get the help we both needed to fight for our marriage and family. After all that thinking and the conversations I had with Curtis, I knew the final straw was to let go. I started to do what I needed to do to start my "moving on" process. Of course, I had mixed feelings about leaving because I didn't want to hurt my kids, but at the same time, I knew I had to put myself first. I hadn't put myself first for twenty-three years.

I ended up moving out on November 1, 2016, and it was the best decision I have made. A huge weight had been lifted off my shoulders. When I say everything fell into place for me, it did and everything came together perfectly. I knew it was nothing but God's plan. When I moved out, all I took from the house were my belongings such as my clothes, my daughter's clothes, my mother's urn and loose end stuff that I bought. I chose not to take any furniture, tv's or electronics. I wanted the transition to be as comfortable as possible for my children in our "family" home. I knew it was going to be hard for them to accept that I moved out and left their Father; therefore, I didn't want the house to look empty. With that being said, I didn't know how I was going to furnish my home, but leaving, with a peace of mind and my sanity, was more important. When I said everything fell into place, it did! My father ended up playing the lottery with my birthdate of 5-2-3, and he hit the number back to back within two weeks. He furnished my entire home! I was so happy and grateful with tears of excitement. That was nothing but GOD!!!!

December, 2016, I was awarded an absolute divorce from Curtis, and I finally felt relieved and proud of myself for doing something that was long overdue. I felt the freedom of having a piece of mind and feeling relieved from a toxic marriage. While at the same time, my three kids struggled with our separating and divorcing, I was hurting for them. One night, I remember going into the new home where my daughter and I were living. I went into my daughter's room, and she was lying in her bed looking really sad with tears in her eyes. I asked her what was wrong, and she said "she didn't know and that she didn't feel right". I then said "is it because you don't live with Dad anymore," and she said "it's just weird, and I know I have to get used to it". I assured her that this adjustment was going to be hard for her and that I would be by her side every step of the way to help her get through it.

My daughter's comment was also one of my biggest inspirations to leave Curtis. One day we were riding in the car, and at this time, she was only eleven years old. I told her I wanted to tell her a secret, and she said "what, you're leaving Dad"? I looked at her as I wasn't expecting her to say that, and I said, "no, why would you say that"? She said, "you just need to leave him, he doesn't deserve you Mommy". I thought that I was shielding her from the noticeable, but she let me know that she knew what I was going through with her Father.

My biggest supporters since day one have been my family, friends and God who have all given me the strength and support to keep moving forward. There were times when I thought about taking my own life to escape the pain and hurt. However, as those thoughts ran through my mind, they quickly went away as I knew it wasn't worth it, and my kids were my strength to rise above the pain and hurt.

I started to think more about life and how precious it is. I learned the power of prayer, and I knew I could get through this and anything else that came my way. I don't wish this experience on anyone, not even my worst enemy. Telling my story was very difficult as the tears kept falling, but it was also my therapy to help deal with my inner pain that I had been shielding for so many silent years. Yes, my smile was visible, but my internal scars were invisible. Staying for the wrong reasons as long as I did, wasn't just because I didn't want to break up my family or hurt my kids, Curtis was all I had known since the age of eighteen. The thought of being with someone else wasn't what I wanted. I allowed him to manipulate me and control my life until I thought such behavior was normal.

I kept telling myself that he was going to change and be the man I deserved, but twenty three years later, he was still the same person. I also believed that I stayed as long as I did because I saw my Mother go through the same kind of unhappy marriage with my Father. I remember seeing my mother sad and crying all the time. The day before she passed away on December 31, 2002, she looked at me and said "Lisa, I know you're not happy, and you deserve so much better, but please promise me that you will not continue to stay with him for the kids". I looked at her and smiled and said, "I won't". Deep down inside I knew it wasn't healthy for me to stay, but I was scared to leave.

I loved this man with everything in me. I stuck by his side through thick and thin and was one hundred percent loyal to him. My miserable and sad days outnumbered my happy days, and that's not how anyone should live life. I loved this man to my core, and I wanted my husband to want me and love me the same way. You can't just love the person you're with; you also need to be in love with them. The happiness of being in love should be mutual. Every day I had to put on a fake smile and pretend that my life was great. When people would ask how I was doing, my response was always "I am doing great" with a smile. I wasn't happy at all. The happily married couple front I had to put on for my family and friends was all for show.

My story isn't just to share with women; it's also for men who may be going through the same thing as I did. I want you to know that it's not okay to stay for the kids, and it's not for their best interest. Consider your happiness and the happiness of your kids. Staying in a toxic situation isn't happiness; it's torture that you and your kids don't deserve. My story is also for couples who may be doing great in their marriage but want to improve and continue to grow within their marriage. Reading my story might make you realize what you can improve by appreciating what you have and valuing it by not taking it for granted and not taking advantage of it.

Throughout my unhealthy marriage, Curtis and I were still blessed and able to raise three amazing, successful children, and I have God to thank for that. As you come to the end of reading my book, I am sure you're saying or thinking to yourself how stupid I was for staying as long as I did and putting up with all the abuse and affairs. As much as I regret the terrible experiences I had to face in those twenty-three years, I can't take it back. However, the fact that I finally had the strength and courage to leave speaks highly of how proud I am of myself. To know my worth as a woman is priceless.

A wise friend always told me that "diamonds are formed from pressure." I have succeeded while shining brightly like a diamond, and I have remained standing tall and smiling after the pain. In the long run, it's not how many times one says sorry or the amount of remorse that truly matters to people who have been hurt. It's stopping the heartbreaking cycle of betrayal that is most essential to their souls. The fear of leaving my husband of twenty-three years and separating my family held me back from doing what I knew was best. We were two people struggling against each other, who got married at a young age, which made it easier for us to grow apart. My husband wasn't willing to change. I realized that he and I didn't have it all together. There were many things that made me also realize that I wanted to be married, but Curtis didn't. At the end of the day, you have to put your family first, and that's something Curtis failed to do for twenty-three years. Once you lose your family, you've achieved nothing.

THIRTEEN
Reality

*"Let go…come to a place of
acceptance and forgiveness."*
-Melissa Trinchet

I fought for so long to keep my family together. Finally, reality set in, and I discovered my worth! Leaving was the hardest decision I've had to make. All I could think about was what my kids would think and feel. They would feel hurt and resentment towards me for leaving their Father. It was heartbreaking for me, but I knew that it was time to think about what was best for them and me. I realized that I would have to teach my children acceptable behavior and the importance of having self worth. I had to be mindful because I didn't want them to not love their Father. His behavior toward me was unacceptable, and I couldn't take it any longer.

When our family and friends on both sides found out about the divorce, some were in shock, but the ones close to me weren't. They saw it coming. As for the ones in shock, their response was, "I had no idea, y'all looked like a perfect, happy couple." My internal response to them was, "yeah, I covered it up with a good act." My response on the outside was "yeah, things happen." When it finally set in that I had divorced Curtis, I started to realize how much I was starting to feel happy, and I began to actually love myself. I realized that I had lived a life for twenty three years that didn't allow me to be myself because I had to uphold this certain image in front of Curtis. It was almost feeling like I was released from prison, and now I was able to finally have freedom to start a new beginning.

My family and friends, as well as Curtis' family members, complimented me on how happy and relieved I looked. Some would say I glowed with excitement. Hearing those words was my validation that I knew I was starting to heal. Although I felt it inside, it was confirmed when I heard compliments from them. What I felt on the inside was showing on the outside; it was magnificent! I remember waking up the next day in my new home feeling like "did this really happen?" "Did I finally get the courage to leave Curtis?"

I was in shock while at the same time, I knew it was nothing but God's plan to make this happen for me. He knew I deserved better. He knew enough was enough, and he blessed me with finding a way out. Reality had set in, and I knew this was going to be challenging for me. At the same time, I knew I had to be strong for my kids. Sometimes, I was devastated inside, and there were times I broke down crying in front of my kids, at work, in front of my family and friends as I felt like I was going through a tragedy. Since the passing of my Mother, this was the second hardest thing I had had to go through. I know you're saying, "how is that when this man treated you terribly?" It was hard for me because the thought of losing my family was devastating.

However, as months went by, and as I was slowly finding my strength and worth as a woman, the more reality had set in with confirmation that Lisa Marie was going to be okay.

Many of us face internal battles that are unknown to others. Those battles seem to be the toughest ones to navigate because we have to face it every day as if nothing is wrong and everything is good. Putting a smile on to mask our pain and hurt is seen far too often. We must learn that removing the mask and revealing how we truly feel is important. We must not forget the importance of tending to our own hearts. At the end of the day when we go home, it's us versus them and no one else. Until we address the underlying issues that cause our heartaches, the hurt will not go away. I wore a smile on my face, but inside, my world was falling apart. When it's all said and done, I will be remembered by how hard I loved.

FOURTEEN
Letting Go

"Choose your happiness over being unhappy."
-Melissa Trinchet

After leaving Curtis in November, 2016 and being in my new home away from the pain, hurt and disrespect, I found myself still in pain with tears of losing my family of twenty three years. Trying to pick up the million pieces to my shattered heart with thoughts of how to literally move on with my life without him was very hard for me. Leaving my husband was like a tragedy with so many mixed emotions. There were times when I wondered if I had made the right decision. I wondered how my kids were feeling, and if I had let them down. What would our family and friends think? I realized that God made this happen the way it was supposed to happen. I realized that my heart wanted to fix Curtis so badly, but I was fighting a losing battle. I was in a situation that I could no longer try to fix.

I mentally kept carrying his actions on as if they were my own burdens. This action was a hindrance that kept me from healing. Sometimes, the reason for letting someone go is because they can't help but hurt you during this phase of their life. When you love deeply, you learn what demons live within them, and you realize that they are hurting you because they are hurting somewhere within themselves. They are fighting a battle within and may not even know it. They take their battles out on you and fight you. Decide to let them go, but not because you're being petty and resentful. You let them go because you really believe that the both of you can find the healing you truly need without being together and hurting each other in the process.

I was attracted to pain like it was a drug. I was addicted to wanting him so much when I knew he didn't want me. Accepting me into his life would have been my healing medicine. I had realized that my toxic relationship held me captive, which stopped me from moving forward. I lost myself and didn't know who Lisa Marie was. I was enabling a bad habit by allowing the cycle of cheating, along with mental and physical abuse, to continue and keep me a captive. His manipulative ways controlled my mind.

Letting someone go doesn't mean you stop loving and caring about him. Letting go means you're choosing freedom over the illusion of loyalty. I smile with being at peace as I finally found the courage to walk away from the pain, the hurt, and heartbreak. I decided to let go, and I chose myself as I discovered my worth. I have adjusted my standards and beliefs. The beauty in my pain is that my story is still being written. Instead of wallowing in my hurt; I found the beauty in what that lesson taught me. I learned to see the good in goodbye!

Tower of Strength

While climbing the tower of strength to get to my happy place in life, I found myself being able to give support and comfort to others in finding their strength. We all go through different things in life that break us, but when you climb that tower of strength, there's no stopping. Finding my strength started with praying and writing in my journal. I didn't lose complete hope as I started to feel my strength through the spirit of courage. I knew I had a heart as loud as a lion, and I no longer wanted my voice to be tamed. So here I am at the top of my tower of strength, putting it all on paper. With strength comes courage, and I refuse to let anyone or anything stop me from sharing my story. I will not apologize for telling my truth. I will not be silent after I have discovered the power of my voice. I was given life because I am strong enough to live it, and my struggles developed my strength.

Sometimes you don't realize your own strength until you come face to face with your greatest weakness. Beliefs have the power to create, and the power to destroy. We have the ability to take any experience in our lives and create a meaning that disempowers us. That same ability can literally save our lives. The true tower of strength is keeping everything together when everyone expects you to fall apart. During my dark moment, when I felt at my lowest with thoughts of taking my life, a bright light from the sun shined upon my face through my basement window.

I felt a spirit telling me to stop letting the devil take over. I immediately got on my knees and prayed the hardest I've ever prayed. I knew my kids needed me as well as my family and friends. So here I am today, standing tall with my head held high with great pride for overcoming such a dark place in my life. In the end, some of my greatest pains have become my greatest "towers of strength".

My Daily Motivation Reads

Birthday card from my Daughter on May 23, 2017

Mom,

You have no idea how much I love and appreciate you. I may not show or express it a lot, but I promise I do. You are the best mother I could ask for, and I wouldn't trade it for anything. You are so supportive and kind, and you make me so happy to be your daughter. I love you so much as a person, and I look up to you very much. I hope to be as nice and as friendly as you! You deserve the world and so much more. I love you so much, Mom. I hope you like your card since I haven't made you one in a while :-). Oh, and HAPPY BIRTHDAY!!!!

Christmas card from my Niece on December 25, 2017

They will insult you, hurt you, defeat you, betray you, injure you, set you aflame and watch you burn, but they will not, shall not, cannot destroy you. You are like Rome, built on ashes, and you are like phoenix and know how to rise and resurrect. You are living proof that you can walk through hell and still be an Angel. When things seem a little hard and when you feel like you want to give up, always remember, you got this! Mason and I, Love You, Merry Christmas, 2017

Valentine's Day card from my Daughter on February 14, 2018

Thank you for being the best mom ever. I appreciate everything you do for me and for everyone else too. You're such a great person, and I love you so much for that. Thank you for always being so thoughtful, and I'm so lucky to be your daughter. I love you so much!

-Your fav daughter

Dear Self,

You have survived a powerful storm, and I couldn't be more proud of you. To overcome the pain and hurt as you learned your worth as a woman, speaks volumes. Days of crying and feeling hopeless felt like it was the end for you as you didn't want to live anymore. Curtis was all you knew, and you believed that you couldn't see your life without him. The problem wasn't him, it was you. You made excuses for his bad behavior; you accepted his obvious lies. Again and again, you gave him another chance. You sold yourself short because you didn't believe you deserved better.

You stayed too long. You learned the hard way, but the blessing is that you LEARNED! As you finally realized how much Curtis wasn't good for you, you chose to pay more attention to yourself and to take care of your inner garden of happiness. You learned to not fall victim to the selfishness of others. You now can live your days to be void of dark moments and the suns of happiness to shine. As you went back and forth about going to see a therapist, and as you thought you could handle it on your own, now you see that leaving was the best decision that you could have made. You needed the guidance and reassurance that you could move on. You needed the confirmation that there is light at the end of the dark tunnel.

Sometimes, in order to be happy, you have to go on an inner journey to heal the wounds of your past. Once you've freed yourself from your fears, it is time to open the eyes of your heart and believe that you truly deserve to be happy. Being strong for your children should be your only focus, as they make you very happy and extremely proud. Despite the up and down emotions your children experienced through the divorce transition, all three of them have continued to do amazing in school and stay focused on living their lives. You showed them the power of strength, and I know they are very proud of you as well.

You now love the person you've become because you fought to become her along with keeping the smile on your face after the pain. Stay true to yourself, and the rest will fall into place as it's meant to be. God has planned everything to work out for your good. You survived because it's your testimony. As you continued to ask God for signs to give you strength, you finally found the strength you've never known. Never be ashamed to tell your story; you lived it – own it! Wear your scars with pride! It's now time for you to detox from the toxic marriage you lived for twenty three years. You are proud of who you are today. Have no more pain as you can breathe and smile again. He's going to be sorry he lost you, so stop worrying. Forget the past, forget the pain and remember what an incredible women you are. You turned your pain into art as the brushstrokes of life became your masterpiece. Lisa Marie, the best is yet to come!

To The Girl Who Hasn't Been
Herself Lately...

*Your spark will return, and you will
shine like you were meant to. It's difficult
when you catch yourself not being you,
and when you feel your whole world
is falling apart before your eyes.*
                                    −Sarah Gordon

Epilogue

A Penny for Your Thoughts

The power of prayer is what I lived by to get through the obstacles I had to face. I don't regret anything I went through, as it was all a learning experience which shaped me into the strong women I am today. My smile finally broke through to the forefront of my pain. As I continue to take baby steps to my happy journey, I've learned that time always heals bad times, and it also teaches us to learn that we should set aside the past and focus on the good things that await us. Writing my first book was an amazing therapeutic experience for me, and I am so happy I didn't give up on writing my story to share it with the world.

Battles I Faced

They say that every person is fighting a battle that the world knows nothing about. I believe this to be true. I was fighting so many battles internally. I recognized the importance of acknowledging those battles that someone else might find healing through their struggle.

The Coverup

The daily smile was my coverup as I hid the internal pain and hurt. After each abuse incident and each affair, I smiled through it all as I didn't want anyone to know how weak I was for continuing to accept this type of behavior from my husband. He didn't value me as his wife nor did he value me as the Mother of his kids. I spoke highly of this man to my family and friends by covering up the mistreatment and disrespect I had to deal with daily. Staying covered up for twenty three years was a norm for me; it was what I was used to, and I settled when I knew in my heart this wasn't the way to be. However, the mask I had been wearing for so long was finally cracking into pieces, and enough was enough.

I Wasn't Enough

I survived eight affairs and maybe more while married to Curtis. My suspicion tells me that there were others that I never knew existed or caught him in during his involvement. Each affair felt like a sharp instrument that chipped into my self worth. My feelings of not being enough were compounded as I found out about each affair. I felt that I just wasn't enough for Curtis even though he tried to assure me that I was more than enough for him. Sometimes, Curtis would question himself because he felt that he didn't deserve someone as beautiful as I was. He would tell me that I had a beautiful heart and that he couldn't understand why I stuck around through all his bullshit. He might have thought that his reassuring gestures and comments would have put me at ease, but they didn't. I questioned myself every day because his actions provoked my feelings of insecurity. I was convinced that I wasn't enough for Curtis.

Lost and Found

Walking away from my marriage for the second time was very hard for me. I loved Curtis, and I loved our beautiful family. I loved our beautiful home that we purchased together for our children. However, I was obsessed with my version of "forever" when I knew in my heart it wasn't real. My marriage sucked the life out of me. I fell madly in love with the wrong person for twenty three years. Am I ashamed? No, not at all! I wear my second divorce from Curtis like a badge of honor. I handed over my broken pieces, and I asked God to please fix me. I've learned to never feel like I'm stuck in a situation because the same way I entered is the same way I can exit. It takes strength and courage to leave.

"You will never look more beautiful than when you stumble from the destruction, and smile at surviving the chaos".
    -Madlyn Beck

Dark Moment

It was May, 2017, that I remember calling my cousin, Catina, crying uncontrollably as my eyes were puffy, and I felt like my life was over. I felt like I couldn't do this anymore. Being alive hurt too much. I was in the fourth month after divorcing Curtis, and I was still grieving due to having to end my marriage for the second time. My kids were hurting from the divorce, and this caused my emotions to be all over the place. As all this was going on, I found out through a mutual friend that Curtis was having an affair with a married woman. This woman was friends with one of my close friends. I felt so disrespected and embarrassed! She lived in the same county and hung out at the same restaurants. We had the same mutual friends. As I sat listening to what my friend was telling me about this affair, I said to myself, "how much more is this asshole going to hurt me with his disrespect?" For him to have an affair with a very well-known, married woman who lived in the same county was beyond mind boggling to me. Was it to get back at me for leaving him? Was this his way of trying to hurt me? Who knows?

The disrespect went as far as him putting this woman in front of our kids. He wouldn't want our daughter to come over to his house because he wanted to have this woman in the house instead. As all this played in my head, the more I felt so disrespected. I did not understand how Curtis could be so heartless and not care how this would affect our kids and me.

This woman's husband came to Curtis' house to confront him about the affair after he blasted Curtis' full name, his home address and a video of Curtis' vehicles on Facebook. This was so embarrassing, and it scared me because of my children. I was concerned for my children's safety because they stay with Curtis sometimes at his house. Curtis kept thinking with the head in his pants and not with the head attached to his shoulders. I was saying to myself "how am I going to face our mutual friends who are all friends with each other?" Since we all had the same mutual friends, everyone started asking me if I knew about the affair. If I went to the mall, a gathering at a friend's house, or to the local restaurant, the affair was being discussed. It was the talk of the town and the gossip of the community. All of the talk, especially among the mutual friends, took a huge toll on me. Our community was small, and news traveled rapidly about Curtis' involvement with this married women.

I experienced much frustration even though I had friends like Catina with whom I could speak to. I remember being in my basement and talking with Catina on the phone. I told her everything as I cried, felt frustrated and angry.

I told her that I didn't want to live anymore. I was at one of the lowest points of my life...I felt weak, and I told her I was tired of being in pain and being hurt. I felt helpless and wanted to end how I was feeling. Catina told me to snap out of it as this was Curtis' issue. She told me to let Curtis deal with it because he was the one acting out because he was hurting inside due to the fact that I finally left his sorry ass. She said you are better than this, and you will rise above it. She reminded me that this was Curtis' embarrassment, not mine at all. She said for Curtis to stoop so low and be that desperate to have an affair with a married woman in the same county revealed his true character. For Curtis to have had an affair in this small community where everyone knew each other was an indication of how much he disrespected you and his family.

She said it was highly disrespectful on so many levels and definitely done out of spite. As I let all of what she said sink in, the more it made me feel better. I was able to snap out of it, and I got stronger day by day with the love and support from my family and friends. Most importantly, the power of prayer and writing my book have been the best therapy for my healing. Catina, thank you for being there every time I called you crying, especially on the day I wanted to give up on life. THANK YOU!!!

My Favorite Cousin

My close relationship with my cousin, David, means everything to me. Watching him grow into a handsome, smart, young man, makes my heart smile with so much joy! I admire his strength; he makes me realize how precious life is. He reminds me to never take anything for granted. David was born with spina bifida that paralyzed him from the waist down. To compare his life with my life made me value mine even more.

His quality of life was limited due to his disability. I remember the day the doctor told us he wouldn't make it past eighteen years old. He was wrong! With God's will, prayers and the day to day amazing care from my aunt and uncle, my cousin is still living. He is thirty four years old and has gone through thirty four surgeries. When David's birthday was coming up, he would ask his Mother if he could walk, and each year it broke my aunt's heart to tell him no. Then one day when David was able to understand, my aunt told him he was born with a disability that caused him to not be able to walk. This was devastating to David as he would see his brother and cousins walk and run around playing while he had to sit in his wheelchair.

I can't imagine how this made him feel, but as his cousin, it broke my heart. His dreams of playing football, basketball or any other sport were shattered, but he didn't let that stop him from being a die hard Redskins fan, basketball, hockey and baseball fan! He loves watching his sports and doing his sport picks with his dad. He loves playing Uno, and he always beats me! HA! David is a ray of sunshine with his handsome smile and his heart of gold. He cares for everyone, and his pleasant demeanor helps him to be able to relate to people. Therefore, if you think life is unfair, think of David. Remember that your situation can always be worse. David, you are my hero and my inspiration. I love you so much!

Letters of Love

Dear Daddy,
 Growing up wasn't always the best, but one thing for sure, I will always be "Daddy's little girl". You and Mommy didn't have the best relationship, but I am not going to sit here and bring back any bad memories. I know how you regret a lot of the decisions you made. I have learned throughout my forty two years on this planet that we must go through some things in life. We must learn from them, and you definitely have learned from your mistakes. We can't take back what has happened; however, we know not to repeat those same mistakes. I am a firm believer that mistakes only make us smarter and wiser. With that said, I salute you, Daddy, for changing for the better!

Thank you for never leaving my side as a child and for never leaving my side during my roller coaster marriage with Curtis. Many times you told me to leave him because he didn't deserve me, but you continued to support me and be there for me. I remember the day I told you that I had finally decided to leave Curtis, and you looked at me and said "Mamita, he never deserved you, and all I want is for you to be happy". I took your advice as it replayed in my head like a song verse. Although I already knew what you told me was true, I knew I had to now accept that I did deserve better. You also said, "We are going to get through this together, and I will be there for you every step of the way".

You have kept your promise. I can never thank you enough for furnishing my new home from top to bottom. I knew it was nothing but God blessing you by making some funds available, not once, but twice back to back!

I remember the day you called me, and you were so excited as you told me to "Get dressed, we're going house shopping!" Daddy, I can't thank you enough or repay you for all that you have done for me and my three children. You are by far the best Father and Grandfather we could ask for. The love you have for us doesn't go unnoticed, and we are very thankful for you every single day. From calling us ten times a day (lol) that gets annoying, we know it's only because we are on your mind all the time. That is a blessing as there aren't a lot of Fathers and Grandfathers like you. Thank you for showering us with your unconditional love and support. I (we) love you with everything!

Love, your Babygirl,
Lisa

"To be a good Mother while my heart was breaking was one of the hardest roles I've ever had to play."
-Melissa Trinchet

Dear Children,

Being pregnant was by far the greatest gift as I carried each of you with so much happiness and great pride. Every time I rubbed my stomach and felt your movement, the more I fell in love. Although each pregnancy was stressful with constant tears due to the pain I endured by staying in an unhealthy marriage, I thank God every day for having three healthy babies. I know first hand what it feels like to have divorced parents. I was twenty three years old when Ma left Papa. I still remember that day like it was yesterday. Even though I was an adult at the time with two kids, I cried like a baby. I remember my stomach feeling so empty, and I lived with a crushed and broken heart. Therefore, I can relate to the pain each of you felt when you found out about the divorce with Dad and I.

I'm sorry things didn't work out with Dad and I as you hoped it would, but I want you to know that I tried to keep our family together. I did all that I could, but when the efforts weren't reciprocated, there wasn't much more that I could have done. I prayed for twenty three years that things would change for the better, but they didn't. God gave me a sign with a way out, and this time I wasn't going to ignore it.

My prayer is that you know your worth and never let an unhealthy relationship take away your happiness. Never allow people to disrespect you with negative words or put their hands on you. When you love someone and care for them, you should treat them the same way you would want to be treated. Never settle and never be afraid to leave a toxic relationship. If a person isn't willing to change, you're not the one for them. People change for whom they want to change. Sadly, it took me twenty three years to realize that I wasn't the one for Dad. I wish things would have been different for us. I wanted us to be that happy family that you deserved, but unfortunately it didn't work out that way. My love for you is greater than my guilt of leaving your Dad as I had to put my happiness first. While I am very sorry for all the "sucky" things that divorce means for you, I have the knowledge of what my collective alternative was. I am unwavering in my decision that this was the best path for all of us. I know this divorce was very hard for you but know that my love and protection for you were demonstrated in giving you a better life.

I wanted to give you a life without tension, arguments and sad moments. When I sat each of you down, before I left Dad to explain why I made the decision to leave, it broke my heart to see the sadness in your faces. At the end of our conversation, you understood and respected my decision to leave.

Mom is free from the pain and hurt, and I'm the happiest I've ever been. Today, I see the happiness in you, and that makes my heart smile with validation that I made the right decision.

Love,
Mom

Dear Mommy,

There's not a day that goes by that I don't think about you. Even though you're not physically here, I feel your spirit with me everyday. So here I am, writing my first book that you inspired me to write - how cool is that? I know you're smiling down on me and feeling so proud of your babygirl. As I was writing this book, my emotions were all over the place. I cried a lot, felt angry and disappointed in myself to have lived the experiences

I wrote about. I felt your wings brush against my face while wiping the tears away. Now that I look back at it, those experiences made me who I am today. I know my strength comes from you, and I can't thank you enough for being the amazing, supportive, Mother you were to me. I know being married to Dad wasn't easy as I remember seeing how unhappy you were. Even though I was at a young age, I was able to understand what was going on. I'm sorry you had to go through that as you didn't deserve it at all. You basically raised four kids on your own, and you did one hell of an amazing job! I salute you and commend you as I am the Mother and strong woman I am today because of you.

You were the glue that kept our family together, and since your passing, I have filled the void with pride. As I close out my letter to you, I want you to know how much I love you and miss you dearly. There are times when I feel weak while needing your guidance to help me get through a situation. I am amazed that you have came through to lift me up every time I've needed you. I feel your spirit guiding me everyday, and it's the best feeling! I pray that you continue to be our guardian Angel watching over us and protecting us with your wings. Until we meet again my beautiful QUEEN...

Dear Curtis,

I left you, and I feel sorry for you because I overlooked your flaws, your temper, your selfishness, and your inability to love anyone but yourself. I could have anyone in the world, but I still chose you every time for twenty-three years. All you are now is a crease in my past, a scar on my chest, a memory that fades faster than a photograph of you in a sealed box, hidden.

the pain behind my smile

I will fight for someone who loves me, instead of someone like yourself who sucked the life out of me. You were never satisfied, even with my beating heart of gold in your greedy hands. I loved you to my core, and as much as you crushed me with disappointment, I will always love you as the Father of our children. I sincerely hope that your soul finds peace. You broke me, but it was only because you were broken. I will heal because I know I need to for me, but I worry that you will never realize that you are in need of healing to deal with the demons you're battling internally.

Thank you for teaching me a lesson of life, for making me realize that I deserve better and for making me strong enough to finally leave a miserable and toxic marriage. I no longer have to hide behind my fake smile. I can finally remove my mask that hid the tears, pain and disappointment. I endured twenty-three years of your constant bullshit, and you never thought I would leave you.

The power of prayer was what finally gave me the courage to leave. You didn't just hurt me and let me down, but our three children were affected tremendously. All they wanted was to have a happy Mother and Father in their home, and they wanted a family that would stay together forever. You broke our family apart because of your selfish actions. You weren't satisfied with just me; you had to keep having affairs to get that extra attention. You couldn't keep your hands to yourself as you felt the need to take your anger out on me. You continued to hurt the person closest to you who loved you, which was me, your wife, the Mother of your kids.

You saw how you were hurting me with your constant affairs, your physical, and verbal abuse, and you belittled me in front of our kids, family and friends. My words have no mercy on you who chose to hurt me and our children repeatedly as deeply as you did. I have no mercy for you as you have no integrity. If I get under your skin, so what? It's because you lack dignity, and you burned right through my skin and scarred my heart for eternity. You repeated how your Mother was mistreated, and mistreated me the same way. You constantly kept shooting me down with each aim you took, but I kept getting back up as your bullets ricochet off my strength. I hope you're proud of yourself for ruining our family. Although you hurt me to my core, sit back and watch me ROAR with happiness like a floating butterfly. I am free from your bullshit!

I forgive you, but that doesn't mean I accept your behavior or trust you. I forgive you for me, so I can LET GO and MOVE ON with my life. I had to step away, not because I didn't care, but because I did too much to let you treat me like I'm less than I'm worth.

About the Author

B orn in Alexandria, Virginia, Melissa is the youngest of four children born to Medin Trinchet and the late Linda Trinchet. She is the proud mother of three children who are her pride and joy! She began her professional career working at the National Institutes of Health in Bethesda, MD from 2001 to present.

Melissa fused her writing with her passion for helping others through her experiences. She is also passionate about helping women and men who ask her for guidance on how to improve their relationship. Although Melissa had to face her family and friends everyday despite the hurt she was feeling inside, she smiled through it. Melissa knows firsthand how it feels to be alone in a marriage. She knew ending her marriage was the best decision she made. Her aspiration in life is to be happy!

Melissa has accepted that everything happens for a reason. She is happy and standing at her conduit of seeing many of her dreams come true.

Connect with Melissa Trinchet on Social Media

instagram .... LisaTMarie
facebook .... Lisa T Marie
email .... melissatrinchet523@gmail.com

www.ingramcontent.com/pod-product-compliance
Lightning Source LLC
Chambersburg PA
CBHW052058070526
44584CB00017B/2236